SOAP

Sarah Woods

SOAP

OBERON BOOKS

LONDON

First published in 2004 by Oberon Books Ltd
521 Caledonian Road, London N7 9RH
Tel: 020 7607 3637 / Fax: 020 7607 3629
e-mail: oberon.books@btinternet.com
www.oberonbooks.com

A catalogue record for this book is available from the British
Library.

ISBN: 1 84002 510 7

To Mum and Dad

With thanks to Laura Harvey, Alan Ayckbourn
and Laurie Sansom

Characters

In Crystal Bay:

THORN, Good-looking in an outdoor way

NOLEEN, Thorn's airhead fiancée

BUNNY, Noleen's hard-bitten mother

LISA (Lis), Thorn's little sister

RON, A handyman

NEALE, A tear-away

PETER, Bunny's father

In Arthur Street:

LORNA, Landlady of the Duke's

JOELY, Lorna's teenage daughter

CHRIS, Lorna's lorry-driving partner

FLOSS, A powerless gossip

MARY, John's mother

JOHN, Lorna's returning ex-husband

ANNABEL, Newcomer barmaid

The action takes place over three episodes.

Notes

A forward slash mark / is used to indicate where characters speak at the same time as one another. This usually applies to immediately consecutive speeches unless otherwise stated in the text.

Where dialogue within a speech starts a new line, this works like a new paragraph in a novel.

The specific doubling of characters is central to the style of this play

Soap was first performed at the Stephen Joseph Theatre, on 16 September 2004, with the following cast:

LORNA, Hannah Waterman

THORN, Ben Hull

PETER / FLOSS, Russell Grant

FLOSS / PETER, Russell Grant

BUNNY/MARY, Susan Twist

NOLEEN/ANNABEL, Sophie Duval

LISA/JOELY, Claire Lams

CHRIS/NEALE, Andrew Brooke

JOHN/RON, Tim Faraday

Director, Laurie Sansom

Designer, Jessica Curtis

Original Music, Anders Sodergren

Lighting Designer, James Farncombe

Stage Manager, Andy Hall

Episode One: Monday

Scene One

The Duke's Head pub, Arthur Street, UK. Morning. JOELY enters, from upstairs, in her school uniform. LORNA follows, in her dressing gown.

LORNA: Where's your coat?

JOELY: I don't need it.

> *She's getting herself ready – maybe putting her hair into a ponytail. LORNA sets up the bar.*

LORNA: What time did you come back last night?

JOELY: Twelve.

LORNA: It was ten to one.

JOELY: So why d'you ask?

LORNA: Are you in for tea?

JOELY: I don't know.

LORNA: Well it'd be useful if you did.

JOELY: What, so you know how many tins of baked beans to open?

LORNA: How are you going to manage at school in this state?

JOELY: That's all you're worried about – what people'll think.

LORNA: I'm worried about you, getting into trouble.

JOELY: Like you care.

LORNA: Of course I care.

JOELY: You don't care about me.

LORNA: How can you say that?

JOELY: Easily.

LORNA: I'm always here for you.

JOELY: You've never cared about me.

LORNA: Where did you go that's upset you like this?

JOELY: Out.

LORNA: What were you drinking?

JOELY: Cups of tea.

LORNA: It would be nice if you could answer one question straight.
You shouldn't even be drinking at your age, and certainly not on weeknights.

JOELY: You want me to tell you the truth?

LORNA: We've always told each other the truth.

JOELY: I don't think you even know the meaning of the word.

LORNA: What's changed? Joely?

JOELY exits through the bar, to her bedroom.

Joely?

LORNA looks puzzled.

Scene Two

The deck of the boat 'The Jack Rabbit', Crystal Bay, Australia. THORN is examining a fishing net on deck. A man and the elements. We hear RON, off.

RON: (*Off.*) Where d'y want this, Thorn?

He enters carrying a wooden bench he's made. THORN helps RON onto the boat with the bench.

THORN: Just here's fine, Ron.

RON starts fixing the bench to the deck and the outside of the cabin with his power tools.

Nice bit of wood.

RON: It is.

THORN: Beer?

RON: Don't mind if I do.

THORN gets a beer from a crate on the deck.

Busy?

THORN: I took a group out first thing.

RON: How's Noleen?

THORN: Ah, she's stoked.

RON: Lovely girl.

THORN: It's all she talks about.

He hands RON a beer – has one himself.

RON: Biggest day of her life.

THORN: Biggest day of mine.
How many d'y reckon you could seat out here?

RON: Thirty – forty at a push. Is that with tables?

THORN: Maybe we should go for a buffet.
Noleen wants about a hundred.

RON: For the wedding?

THORN: The reception.

RON: Don't think you'll get a hundred on the Jack Rabbit, mate.

THORN: No. She wants a big do.

RON: So I've heard.

THORN: It'd mean a lot to me to have it on the Jack Rabbit.

RON does some drilling.

RON: Heard something you might not want to know.

THORN: What?
What is it Ron?

RON: Just don't shoot the messenger.
Neale Bolton's back.

THORN: Neale Bolton.

RON: Got out at the weekend, came straight back down here.
I saw him catching some surf.

THORN: That isn't all he'll be catching if he stays down here.

RON: Strike a light, mate, I'm only telling you.
Anyway, who says he hasn't changed now he's back home?

THORN: I'd bet the Jack Rabbit on it.

We hold the image of THORN, angry, looking out to sea, beer in hand.

Scene Three

The Duke's Head. LORNA answers the door to CHRIS, he enters.

CHRIS: What's up?

LORNA: Joely just had a real go at me.

CHRIS: She's sixteen, what d'you expect?

LORNA: She didn't come home 'til nearly one this morning.

CHRIS: So she's tired.

LORNA shouts up the stairs to JOELY.

LORNA: Joely?

CHRIS: Stop fretting.

LORNA: It's not like her.

CHRIS takes LORNA's face in his hands.

CHRIS: Everything'll be okay.

LORNA: Are you coming for tea?

CHRIS: Lunch, tea – I can't stay away, Lorna.

They kiss.

LORNA: I've got that woman to interview at eleven.

CHRIS: You'll be able to take a bit of time off once you've got another barmaid.

LORNA: I just hope she's okay. She's the only person applied.

CHRIS: I'll pop in around one.

LORNA: What about your tender?

CHRIS: I've done all their haulage for three years – that must count for something.

LORNA: I wouldn't bet on it.

CHRIS: I'm the only haulage business round here.

JOELY storms through.

Do you want a lift, Joely?

JOELY slams a locket on the counter before leaving with a big bag. She pushes past FLOSS, who's on her way in with her shopping trolley, and exits. LORNA picks up the locket, tearful.

FLOSS: (*After JOELY.*) Morning to you too.

Charming.

LORNA: She left her locket.

FLOSS: That's not Joely's locket is it?

LORNA: She never takes it off.

FLOSS: She hasn't taken it off, has she?

CHRIS: Perhaps she didn't want to lose it.

LORNA: She wears it in the bath.

FLOSS: She hasn't taken it off, slammed it down on the bar and stormed out, has she?

CHRIS: What if she has?

FLOSS: Next thing you know she'll be telling you she's having a baby – or you're having a baby –

She narrows her eyes at CHRIS.

You haven't been sleeping with Joely, have you?

CHRIS: No!

FLOSS homes in on the locket.

FLOSS: Someone's doing something to someone or something's happened that shouldn't.
It's a start, that's what that is.
I'll get my bucket.

FLOSS goes through to the toilets, taking her trolley with her.

CHRIS: Perhaps the clasp's broke.

LORNA: You heard what Floss said.

CHRIS: Floss doesn't know everything.

LORNA looks at the locket. CHRIS looks at LORNA, concerned.

Scene Four

Bunny's Café, Crystal Bay. RON enters from outside carrying a wooden archway. NOLEEN comes out from behind the counter, carrying a shoebox.

RON: You know where your mum wants this?

He indicates the archway.

NOLEEN: Right here, I think.

RON: I better check with her. Don't want to get myself in trouble.

NOLEEN is absorbed getting high-heeled white shoes out of the box – out of earshot of the ensuing conversation.

Bunny!

BUNNY comes through the door behind the counter. She wears a short-sleeved top and has 'NOLEEN' tattooed onto her arm.

BUNNY: Thought you'd forgotten me, Ron.

RON: How could I?

BUNNY: Just here.

She wants the archway in the gap between two halves of the counter.

All eyes'll be on this place on Friday, Ron. And I'm going to make sure some of them are on me.

RON: It's the talk of the bay.

BUNNY: It's an important day for all of us, Ron.

RON: You done good with Noleen.

BUNNY: My little girl getting hitched.

RON: Can't say I would've thought it when you first caught with her.

BUNNY: Not what I had in mind, but.

RON: Never thought she'd survive a day never mind see her
growed up and married.
Didn't exactly have you down as homespun.

BUNNY: We all have our roles to play.

RON: And then when Ted left you.

BUNNY: It's all coming good.

RON: Who'd have thought a juice stand on the beach'd turn
into this.

BUNNY: It all comes, Ron.

RON: Bunny's Café.

BUNNY: Just a matter of waiting. This wedding's going to
be just perfect.

RON: Good of you to put them up and all, Bunny.

BUNNY: Not for long, Ron. If everything goes according to
my little plan, it'll soon be just the three of us again.

RON: The three of us?

BUNNY: Me, myself and I, Ron.

NOLEEN shows RON her shoes.

NOLEEN: What'dy think, Ron?

RON: Streuth, they're real bobby-dazzlers – not quite the
thing for wearing on a boat, though.

NOLEEN: I'm not wearing them on a boat.

RON: I thought you were having this wedding reception of
yours on the Jack Rabbit.

NOLEEN: What?

RON: That's what Thorn told me.

NOLEEN: The Jack Rabbit?

She looks at BUNNY in panic.

Mum?

BUNNY: Course you're not, darling, you're having it right here.

RON: Mind you, you won't get more than forty on there –

NOLEEN: He hasn't said anything to me.

RON: Maybe fifty with a buffet, and God help you if anyone falls off.

BUNNY: It's not going to happen.

NOLEEN: Fifty? Fifty's not half enough.

BUNNY: Where is Thorn?

RON: Might need to get everyone in life jackets.

BUNNY: Don't want him going AWOL between now and Friday.

NOLEEN: Course he won't go AWOL.

BUNNY: Where's he got to?

RON: Gee, he loves that boat.

BUNNY: It's my daughter he's marrying, Ron.

RON: Sure thing, Bunny – I was just saying.

BUNNY: Not some lump of wood.

As RON puts up the archway with his power drill, THORN enters from outside.

Here he is.

THORN: Hiya sweetheart.

NOLEEN and THORN embrace, he kisses her.

NOLEEN: I missed you.

THORN: Missed you too.

RON does a bit of drilling – continuing intermittently through the scene – sometimes making it hard for the other characters to talk.

NOLEEN: I've decided on the cake.

THORN: It's going to be fantastic.

NOLEEN: I'm having the people on the top – but not the man in the top hat. The man in the suit.

THORN: I mean the rest of our lives.

NOLEEN: It's got three tiers.

THORN: We can go anywhere –

NOLEEN: And really real icing flowers.

THORN: Get what we want.

NOLEEN: You're what I want, Thorn.

THORN: I mean out of life. Just get on the Jack Rabbit and go. Maybe if we go far enough and look hard enough, we might find Mum.

THORN looks into the middle distance at the thought of his Mum.

NOLEEN: I thought we were going to Bali?

THORN: Noleen, we need to talk –

NOLEEN: If it's about having the reception on the Jack Rabbit –

THORN: It won't work, sweetheart. It's just not big enough.

NOLEEN: Oh.

THORN: No matter how much we want it, we won't get a hundred on there.

NOLEEN: A hundred and thirty.

THORN: A hundred and thirty?

NOLEEN: There were a few I forgot.
I should have known you'd understand.

THORN: But it would be perfect for the wedding.

BUNNY is listening.

There's only forty people coming for the ceremony – if that. Just family – I haven't really got any apart from Lis and she doesn't take up much room.

NOLEEN: Mum –

THORN: It's perfect. Out in the open air, on the open waves.

NOLEEN: At sea?

BUNNY: No worries, love.

NOLEEN: Get married at sea?

BUNNY: You can get married anywhere these days –

NOLEEN: It'll all be rocking about.

RON: You could do it in the sea!

NOLEEN: What about my shoes –

RON: Get the vicar in his swimmers.

BUNNY: How romantic.

RON: Thorn looks good in a wetsuit.

THORN: You up for it, Noleen?

BUNNY: Course she is.

RON: Let's give it a burl –

NOLEEN: Mum!

BUNNY: If it wasn't for Granddad, we'd all go for it.

NOLEEN: Granddad?

RON: Peter?

THORN: What do you mean, Bunny?

BUNNY: Granddad won't be going on the Jack Rabbit again.

THORN: But it was his boat.

BUNNY: He's having enough trouble with his land legs these days, never mind his sea legs.

THORN: He's never said anything to me.

RON: Me neither.

BUNNY: Of course he hasn't said anything. Just like he doesn't say anything about his house.

THORN: What's wrong with his house?

BUNNY: It's too big for him. He can't keep it up.

THORN: Looks all right to me.

BUNNY: That's exactly what he wants you to think. Old man like him shouldn't be rattling around in a great place like that.

RON: Seems happy enough to me.

RON has finished the arch and now examines the counter, which he thinks needs work.

BUNNY: I grew up in that house. It needs a family.

She shoots a look at NOLEEN.

That's a family house, that is.

NOLEEN smiles a little.

A little sheltered place, that's what he wants.

THORN: Peter?

RON: What about his veggies – where would he grow them?

THORN: I don't think he's quite ready to be put out to pasture yet, Bunny.

BUNNY: He's no spring chicken. He's seventy-six years old.

RON: I thought he was sixty-seven.

BUNNY: Seventy-six.

THORN: Seems all right to me.

BUNNY: Needs a bit of specialist care.

THORN: He'd love us getting married on the Jack Rabbit.

BUNNY: It was a big day for all of us when he gave you the Jack Rabbit, Thorn. Don't you think getting married on his old boat's a bit rich, when his sea legs have reached the end of their usefuls?

RON: Where is he, anyway?

BUNNY: Peter?

THORN: Haven't seen him for a while.

RON: Neither have I, come to think of it.

BUNNY: He's got to go to Brisbane.

THORN: Peter?

RON: Brisbane?

THORN: When?

BUNNY: Wednesday.

RON: Streuth.

NOLEEN: He'll be back for the wedding, but?

THORN: Bunny?

BUNNY narrows her eyes and looks away.

Bunny?

BUNNY exits behind the counter.

NOLEEN: Can I get you a coffee, Thorn?

RON: Thorn?

THORN: Doesn't matter.

NOLEEN: Shall I get you that coffee?

THORN: Coffee, juice – doesn't really matter.

NOLEEN: But you always drink coffee.

THORN: Do I?

NOLEEN: Black and strong with / one sugar.

RON: One sugar.

THORN: I'll have a smoothie.

We hold the image – THORN looking into the middle distance, moody. NOLEEN concerned, RON thinking about drilling.

Scene Five

LISA sits on the beach, looking out to sea. NEALE walks up – fresh from the sea in wetsuit and carrying a surfboard, dripping.

NEALE: Didn't know I had an audience.

LISA: Sorry – I wasn't watching really.
How are the waves?

NEALE: The waves are fine, it's me needs more practice.

LISA: Looked all right to me.

NEALE: I need a bit of a breather. I haven't been down here for a while.
Hasn't changed much, has it?

LISA: Nothing much changes here.

NEALE: I haven't seen you before.

You live here?

LISA: Yeah.

NEALE: Been here long?

LISA: All my life.
How about you?

NEALE: Long time ago.
Seems like a very long time ago.
I'm Neale.

LISA: Lisa.
So why come back?

NEALE: Where else is there?

LISA: This bit of coast isn't the whole world.

NEALE: It's always been my world.
What do you do?

LISA: I'm at school. Year Twelve.

NEALE: School's still going then?

LISA: Never stops.

NEALE: And the café – Bunny's?

LISA: Yeah.

NEALE: Course it is. I might pop in there this arvo. Maybe about four o'clock?

LISA: Okay.

He starts to go back to the sea.

NEALE: Maybe catch you later.

LISA: (*To herself.*) Yeah.
Later.

She picks up her bag. Walks off a little way, then turns and looks back. Her hair is blown by the sea breeze. She holds her hand up to her eyes to shield them from the sun as she looks out to sea.

Scene Six

MARY's back door, Arthur Street. LORNA has her coat on. She knocks. After a few moments, MARY opens it.

LORNA: Mary –

MARY: Lorna.

LORNA: It's Joely. She's disappeared. Taken some of her stuff – clothes and her school books. Something happened last night that's really upset her.

LORNA looks at the locket in her hand.

LORNA: She left her locket.

MARY: The locket you gave her when John left?

LORNA: You haven't seen her, have you?

MARY: She's decided to stay with me for a bit.

LORNA: What?

MARY: I've given her one of my Bed and Breakfast rooms.

LORNA: What's this all about?

MARY: I can't tell you, Lorna.

LORNA: It's something bad, isn't it?

MARY: She's waiting for her father to ring her back.

LORNA: John? What's she speaking to John about?

MARY won't answer.

We haven't clapped eyes on him for the last decade and a half, why on earth does she want to talk to him?

MARY: That's between him and her.

LORNA: What does she think he's going to do? If he had any interest in Joely, he'd have come back by now.

MARY: You know that, do you?

LORNA: We both know it, Mary. He couldn't get out of here fast enough. Nothing's going to get him back. Admit it, Mary. We're all Joely's got.

JOELY appears, behind MARY.

JOELY: What's she doing here?

LORNA: Joely!

As LORNA tries to move in and get hold of JOELY, JOELY moves away, exiting.

MARY: Leave it, Lorna.

LORNA: I want to talk to her.

MARY: She won't talk to you.

LORNA: She's always talked to me. She said her first words to me.
I need to know what's wrong with her.

MARY: Perhaps if you cast your mind back, you might think of something.

LORNA: I only said she shouldn't be out drinking on a school night.

MARY: Listen Lorna, I'm not going to cast judgement until I know the facts –

LORNA: So tell me what's going on.

MARY: Only you know the answer to that.

LORNA: How can I know the answer if I don't even know the question?

MARY: I don't think we should be having this conversation.

LORNA: She left this.

She indicates the locket.

She's rung John.

MARY: I'm not going to stand here arguing the toss with you, Lorna.

LORNA: She's my daughter.

MARY: And John's my son.

LORNA: How long have we known each other, Mary? You've been like a mother to me. I haven't got any secrets from you. You know me.

MARY: I thought I knew you.

LORNA: You do. You know all there is to know.

MARY: Sometimes people aren't who you think they are.

LORNA: Who do you think I am?

MARY: I'm not sure at the moment, Lorna. And I don't think Joely is either.

LORNA: I'm a good mother. You know that.

MARY: Do I?

LORNA: You've said I'm a good mother. You're always saying it. You and me. What are we if we're not good mothers, Mary?

MARY: Leave it, Lorna.

LORNA: I wouldn't do anything to hurt Joely.

JOELY appears again.

Joely.

JOELY: I don't want to talk to her.

LORNA: Look at me.

MARY: She doesn't want to talk to you.

LORNA: I don't have to take this, Mary –

MARY: Leave her.

LORNA: We belong together.

JOELY: I don't.

LORNA: We've always been together.

JOELY: I can't get far enough away from you.

LORNA: I'm your mum.

MARY: That's enough.

LORNA: That's who I am.

JOELY: If you were on the other side of the planet, you'd still be too close.

LORNA: That's why I've done everything I've done.

JOELY: I don't want anything from you.

LORNA holds out the locket.

LORNA: At least take your locket.

A moment, then JOELY takes it.

MARY: (*To LORNA.*) Go on.

LORNA turns away from the door and begins to move away. JOELY throws the locket after her – it lands in the street.

LORNA: What have I done?

MARY shuts the door. LORNA crouches down and picks up the locket. She looks at it, crouched on the floor. FLOSS enters with her shopping trolley.

FLOSS: Who threw that.
Joely?

LORNA: She hasn't taken it off since she was big enough to put it on herself – before that she kept it under her pillow.

FLOSS: It doesn't matter what's already happened.

LORNA: Of course it matters.

FLOSS: It's what's going to happen next is important.

LORNA: If all that matters is what happens next, how can we know anything?

FLOSS: Things change. People change.

LORNA: I haven't changed.

FLOSS: I used to be a real imp – men at my feet, never less than two of them on the go.
'Til I got married, then I was never outside the front door except to buy a pint of milk.

LORNA: I've always been the same.

FLOSS: Then a bitch, manipulating my man into the grave. And now I don't get the men anymore. I get a dog and a mental health problem, a few laughs if I'm lucky. It's not much fun getting old. But better than being dead.

LORNA: I've always been the same.

FLOSS: You have to reinvent yourself.
I never stop. Even when I'm asleep I'm changing. That's how much it takes.

LORNA: I don't want to be anyone else.

FLOSS: I might try shoplifting.
Or that thing with your – you know – that – saying the wrong worms. 'Beef burglars and chips' –
'Don't throw the bath-water out with the baby'.
Or go all forgetful: Who are you?

LORNA: Lorna.

FLOSS: How old are you?

LORNA: Thirty.

FLOSS: When did John leave?

LORNA: Fifteen years ago.

FLOSS: How old's Joely?

LORNA: Sixteen.

FLOSS: She's never sixteen. How old were you when you had her?

LORNA: Twenty.

FLOSS: Doesn't add up, does it?

LORNA: It must.

FLOSS: You should have an affair.

LORNA: I've always been Lorna.

FLOSS: A torrid affair.

LORNA: I don't want an affair.

FLOSS: You better do something. Before something does you.

FLOSS toddles off with her trolley.

Scene Seven

Bunny's Cafe, Crystal Bay. THORN is sitting at the counter, which RON is making some improvements to. LISA enters.

THORN: Hi sis, what you doing here?

LISA: I'm meeting someone.

NOLEEN: Anyone we know?

LISA: I don't think so.

NOLEEN: What can I get you?

LISA: An OJ thanks, Noleen.

NOLEEN gets her one.

RON: Not more young love, is it? Jeez, I'm just about stifled with the stuff in here as it is.

BUNNY: Don't be such a killjoy. Just coz you're past it.

RON: Young love? Streuth. Give me old love any day. You both know what you're there for, and there's no danger of getting her up the spout.

LISA: He's just a friend.

NOLEEN takes LISA her OJ. NEALE enters.

Hi.

She goes over to him and they sit down together. THORN stands up.

THORN: (*Under his breath.*) Neale Bolton. Hasn't changed a bit.

NOLEEN: What?

RON: That's Neale Bolton, darl.

BUNNY: Well I never.

NOLEEN: The one who –

THORN: Dead right.

RON: So they say.

NOLEEN: He went away for it, didn't he?

BUNNY: Certainly did.

THORN: Flamin' mongrel.

NOLEEN: What's he doing here?

RON: He's just got out.

THORN: Back to the scene of his crime.

LISA and NEALE laugh together. THORN goes to go over – but NOLEEN holds his arm.

NOLEEN: They're only talking.

THORN: They might be only talking today –

NOLEEN exits behind the counter to fetch someone's order. LISA and NEALE laugh again.

BUNNY: Take it easy, Thorn.

We tune into LISA and NEALE's conversation as THORN goes over.

NEALE: So I gave him the hard hat back –

LISA: Didn't he ask where the horse was?

NEALE: No need. It was standing right next to him. Beaten me to it. So I thought maybe horse-riding wasn't for me. I'm more comfortable behind the bars of a motorbike.

THORN: What about the bars of a prison cell?

NEALE: Thorn –

THORN: That's where you've been these last four years.

LISA: Neale?

NEALE: Remand Centre – it was a Remand Centre.

THORN: That sound better, does it, sis?

NEALE: Lisa – I was going to tell you.

THORN: Sure.

NEALE: I've done my time.

THORN: Why don't you get out?

NEALE: I haven't finished my juice.

THORN: Get out, Neale.

NEALE: You don't own this café, do you?

BUNNY: No. I do.
    And I don't want any trouble.

NEALE: I'm just taking the weight off my feet and drinking
    a juice.

LISA sits down.

BUNNY: He ain't doing nothing wrong, Thorn.

THORN: You got a light, Neale?

NEALE: I don't smoke.

THORN: No, just everything around you.

LISA: What?

THORN: Come on, Lis.

LISA: I'm drinking my juice.

THORN: I'm not happy about this, Lis.

LISA: You don't have to be.

THORN: You're worth more than this.

NEALE: (*To LISA.*) You better go.

*LISA gets up. THORN and LISA walk out. NEALE bangs
his fist on the table.*

Scene 8

The Duke's Head, Arthur Street. LORNA is interviewing ANNABEL.

ANNABEL: Whose is the lorry outside?

LORNA: My partner's.

ANNABEL: Chris Haines?

LORNA: Do you know him?

ANNABEL: Says it on the side of the truck.

LORNA: Have you done bar work before?

ANNABEL: No. But I've had plenty of practice pouring drinks.

LORNA: Pints?

ANNABEL: Shorts mainly, but I'm versatile.
I seem to be able to turn my hand to most things.

LORNA: So where were you before?

ANNABEL: Before I came here?

LORNA nods.

I was at home. I came straight over.

LORNA: I meant a job.

ANNABEL: I've never worked before. Haven't needed to.
So is Chris going for the Hughes tender, then?

LORNA: Yeah.

ANNABEL: Worried, is he?

LORNA: Not really. He's the only haulage business round here.

ANNABEL: Except for Fripp and Son on the Industrial Estate down Queensway.

LORNA: What Industrial Estate?

ANNABEL: Past the canal.

LORNA: I didn't know there was an Industrial Estate down Queensway.

ANNABEL: Then there's Sharp Haulage up Roseberry Hill. You must have heard of them.

LORNA: No.

LORNA gives ANNABEL a glass.

ANNABEL: Mal Sharp?

LORNA: Chris's never mentioned them.

ANNABEL: Big man, dark, quite built. At least he likes to think he is.

LORNA: Make sure the tap stays in the beer as much as possible.

ANNABEL starts to try and pull a pint.

ANNABEL: What's it like running this place?

LORNA: It's all right.

ANNABEL: You do it on your own?

LORNA: For the last fifteen years, since my husband left.

The beer tap gurgles and spits.

ANNABEL: Looks like you need to change the barrel.

LORNA: I've never known it run out before.

ANNABEL: You must've changed a barrel in fifteen years.

LORNA: Not that I can remember.

ANNABEL: Do you want me to go down – I'm sure I'd manage.

LORNA: I can manage.

ANNABEL: I've always fancied running a pub.

LORNA: I can do it.

ANNABEL: So have I got the job?

LORNA: If you want it, yes.

ANNABEL: I'll start now if you want to change that barrel. Don't worry – you can trust me.

LORNA goes into the cellar. ANNABEL smiles a wicked smile – there's more to her than meets the eye.

Scene Nine

Crystal Bay, the deck of the Jack Rabbit. LISA and NEALE enter.

LISA: D'you want a drink?

NEALE: Won't he notice stuff's gone?

LISA: He knows I come here. I hang out here quite a lot.

NEALE: On your own?

LISA: Yeah.

NEALE: It's great.

LISA: Him and Noleen are looking at flowers for the wedding.

NEALE: They always were going to get hitched, weren't they?

LISA: Yeah.

NEALE: I remember them when I was at school.
Real grown-up they seemed then.
We don't have to do this, you know. If us spending time together's making problems between you and Thorn.

LISA: It's Thorn's problem.

NEALE: You don't even know what I did.

LISA: You'll tell me. When you're ready.

NEALE: He's had the boat a while, then?

LISA: It was Noleen's Granddad's.
We used to go out on it all the time when we were kids.
And we came here when Mum was – when she wasn't around.
The Jack Rabbit's always been here.

NEALE: About earlier, what Thorn said –

LISA: I don't want to know. I mean it Neale. Tell me because you want to, not because you think you have to. This is nothing to do with anyone else.

NEALE: Didn't look like that in the café.

LISA: He's just trying to take care of me.

NEALE: I can see that.

LISA: He looks after me. Since Mum…

NEALE: What happened?

LISA: She disappeared.

NEALE: Sounds like my Mum. Drove out there and never came back.

LISA: In the bush. They went out bush-walking. There was a fire.

NEALE: Jeez.

LISA: We looked for her. Thorn did. I was only eight. Everyone looked for her. They found her jeep with a flat. Never found her body. She just never came home.

NEALE: I remember hearing about it.

LISA: People said maybe she'd got lost, trying to get home. For years we thought she'd come back. Used to hear her coming in the front door. Just about stopped listening now.
Thorn's the only one. The only one who's been there for me. It's just he forgets I'm out of nappies sometimes.

NEALE: You've not got anyone? Like Thorn's got Noleen.

LISA shakes her head.

Most likely Thorn puts them off.

LISA: Most likely me puts them off.

NEALE: Nah.
You haven't put me off.

LISA: Give me time.

He takes her hand.

NEALE: I've got time.

They kiss. THORN enters. They spring apart. Hold – them looking at him. Him looking at them.

LISA: Thorn.

THORN: Lisa.

Scene 10

Arthur Street. The Duke's. ANNABEL is behind the bar. FLOSS enters.

ANNABEL: Don't tell me, a dry sherry.

FLOSS: Sweet. Who are you?

ANNABEL: I could ask you the same question.

FLOSS: I asked it first.

ANNABEL: I'm Annabel.

ANNABEL gives her her drink.

FLOSS: Floss.
You're trouble, aren't you?

ANNABEL: Don't worry – not for you.

FLOSS tastes her drink.

FLOSS: This isn't sherry.

ANNABEL: Things aren't always what they seem, are they?

CHRIS enters.

(*To CHRIS.*) What would you like?

CHRIS: Where's Lorna?

ANNABEL: Popped out.

CHRIS: You the new barmaid?

ANNABEL: The beer's off, but we've got bottles.

CHRIS: I don't drink.

ANNABEL: I pour a lovely scotch on the rocks.

CHRIS: Orange juice.

ANNABEL: Shall I pop a vodka in that?

FLOSS: Chris doesn't drink.

CHRIS: I don't drink.

ANNABEL: How's the tender?

CHRIS: How do you know about that?

ANNABEL: My boyfriend's up for it. Mal Sharp. Sharp Haulage.

CHRIS: Never heard of them.

ANNABEL: He's the name on everyone's lips after Eddie Stobart.

CHRIS: Where's Lorna?

ANNABEL: She's gone to change the barrel.

FLOSS: In the cellar?

ANNABEL: Yes.

FLOSS: On her own?

ANNABEL: She's only in the cellar. It's not like she's started a new life somewhere.

CHRIS: What do you mean started a new life somewhere?

ANNABEL: I said she hasn't started a new life somewhere.

FLOSS: You know that do you? How long's she been gone?

ANNABEL: I don't know – ten minutes.

FLOSS goes to have a look.

Perhaps she's got someone down there.

CHRIS: What do you mean?

ANNABEL: Some people's reputations go before them.

CHRIS: What reputation?

ANNABEL looks at him, raising an eyebrow. CHRIS walks out.

FLOSS: You don't mess about, do you?

ANNABEL: I like to keep active.

FLOSS: Keeps you young.

ANNABEL: Only hope I look as good as you when I'm your age.

FLOSS: I keep very active. Very active.

FLOSS sips her sherry, thoughtful. ANNABEL polishes a glass.

Scene Eleven

Set back to THORN standing looking at LISA and NEALE on the boat.

LISA: Thorn.

THORN: Rack off.

THORN picks up a beer.

LISA: What've we done?

THORN: I'm not talking to you, Lis.

LISA: You can't do this.

NEALE: Don't worry, I'm going.

LISA: No –

NEALE: I don't need the aggro, Lis.

NEALE exits.

LISA: I don't believe this.

She starts to go after him.

THORN: Where are you going?

LISA: I'm going with him.

LORNA appears, blinking, out of the cabin of the Jack Rabbit. She has no idea where she is, but realising she's stumbled into a private scene, she tries not to get in the way. She listens, watches.

THORN: Lisa, don't go.

LISA: Just because you don't like him.

THORN: Nor would you if you knew about him.

LISA: Wouldn't I?

THORN: He hasn't told you, has he?

LISA: He doesn't have to.

THORN: The dag set the school on fire.

LISA: Maybe it was an accident.

THORN: On parents' evening? Everyone inside. Torched it with petrol.

LISA: I don't want to know.

THORN: I bet you don't.

THORN notices LORNA, LORNA smiles, a little embarrassed. THORN continues with the scene.

Changes the picture a bit, doesn't it?

LISA: It doesn't change anything.

THORN: Why do you think someone does something like that?

LISA: Maybe because they're having a hard time.

THORN: Arson's going to help.

LISA: It was ages ago.

THORN: He was old enough to know better.
I just don't want things getting out of hand between you and him, Lis.

LISA: I'm sixteen.

THORN: And you know everything, do you?

LISA: Maybe he's changed.

THORN: Don't mind if I reserve judgement?
I was at the school that night.

LISA: No-one was killed.

THORN: He was lucky. Lucky not to be up on a murder charge. Maybe it would have been better if he was.

LISA: Better for who?

THORN: Better for you, Lis.

LISA: No, Thorn, better for you. This is your problem.

LISA has a look at LORNA, LORNA's engrossed in the scene.

THORN: You're my sister, Lis. I'm your brother. And like it or not, I'm all you've got.

LISA: Do you think you have to remind me of that?

THORN: I don't want you to see him again.

LISA: Fine.

LISA is leaving, she bumps into LORNA.

LORNA: Sorry –

LORNA tries to get out of the way.

THORN: Do you hear me?

LORNA: Sorry.

LISA exits.

THORN: Lis!

THORN tries to maintain his pose – looking into the distance, hurt – but is drawn to LORNA. The lights come on in The Duke's on another part of the stage, revealing FLOSS nursing a sherry at the bar. ANNABEL is behind the bar. JOHN enters.

JOHN: Any chance of getting a drink around here?

LORNA seems oblivious to the Arthur Street scene. She looks at THORN. They gaze into each other's eyes.

FLOSS: John Dove.

JOHN: Floss.

FLOSS: What are you doing back?

ANNABEL is flirtatious with him.

ANNABEL: Sounds like I should know who you are.

CHRIS enters and comes to the bar, shocked to see JOHN.

FLOSS: Come to take your daughter away with you, maybe?

JOHN: Where's Lorna?

Still looking at each other, THORN gives LORNA his beer bottle.

FLOSS: Or to take Lorna away with you.

LORNA smoothes her hair down. She should be on by now.

ANNABEL: What can I get you?

JOHN: I'll wait for Lorna.

FLOSS: Or to take me away with you.

CHRIS: What do you want?

JOHN: This is a pub. I want a drink.

LORNA realises she should be somewhere else.

LORNA: Excuse me –

LORNA runs into the cabin of the Jack Rabbit. THORN is left in his still image, trying not to move. Arthur Street waits for LORNA. CHRIS looks at JOHN. JOHN looks at CHRIS. FLOSS looks at JOHN. ANNABEL looks at CHRIS. CHRIS looks at the counter.

THORN frowns and looks at the cabin. LORNA enters the Duke's through the cellar door – the same way she just went out – flustered and ruffled. She puts the Australian beer down on the counter. Lights down on Crystal Bay. In Arthur Street, all eyes are on LORNA and JOHN.

LORNA: John.

JOHN: Lorna.
Long time and all the rest of it.

LORNA: What do you want?

JOHN: That would be telling.

CHRIS glares at JOHN. JOHN looks at LORNA. ANNABEL looks at CHRIS.

Episode 2: Wednesday

Scene One

The signature tune for Crystal Bay *begins. We watch the following vignettes take place all round the stage – so we have to turn to see the next one. They're always moving, a continual well-practiced flow. We see: NOLEEN run on, chased by THORN. He catches her. She hits him playfully. He holds her. She runs off again, leaving him. He stands, looking into the middle distance – he frowns slightly.*

PETER with a spade. He is about to dig, then stops. Looks up – he's seen someone. He salutes them and laughs. They go. He wipes his brow and cocks his head to one side. All's right with the world.

RON – about to drill something. He turns his head – pauses – and looks into the middle distance.

BUNNY walks on with a coffee in one hand and a piece of cake on a plate in the other. She catches an unseen customer's eye and walks, as if over to them holding out their order.

Scene Two

Crystal Bay. Outside Bunny's Café. PETER is surrounded by all his belongings. BUNNY is adding his armchair to the pile.

PETER: Seen it all before, mate. Good looking young bloke.

NOLEEN: (*Off.*) What about these photo albums?

BUNNY: Yes.

> *BUNNY exits as NOLEEN enters, with more things, including the photo albums.*

PETER: Marries childhood sweetheart.
Wife dies in terrible accident.

> *NOLEEN gives him more.*

NOLEEN: All right, Granddad?

NOLEEN exits.

PETER: Left to bring up their daughter. Gets old and no-one's interested anymore.
No-one's interested in your hobbies, your one-liners, your life experience.

THORN: You want to get out a bit more, Peter.

PETER: I'd like to.

THORN: Just wish mum could be here to see me getting hitched.

BUNNY brings on more of PETER's things – maybe including some veggies, cabbages, seeds, or a tray of seedlings. She shouts to NOLEEN, who is off stage.

PETER: I know, Thorn.

BUNNY: That's the lot, Nols.

BUNNY dumps the last of his stuff.

Time for the bus in a mo, Dad.

She goes.

THORN: People said maybe when the jeep broke down she got lost, trying to get home.
She's out there somewhere, Peter. Wandering around in the dust and the heat. Looking for us. Waiting for me to find her and bring her back.

PETER: Maybe she doesn't want to come back.

THORN: Of course she wants to come back. It was the first time she'd worn that dress.

PETER: Maybe she took the chance to get out while the going was good.

THORN: Mum loved that dress.

PETER: Before it got too late.
Do you know how old I am, Thorn?

THORN: About as old as you feel, I reckon.

PETER: I thought I was sixty-seven.

THORN: I don't know, mate.

PETER: The November before last. When I had my birthday. You remember that. I was sixty-five.

THORN: Were you?

PETER: I had a party. It was a surprise.

THORN: For your seventy-fifth?

PETER: Sixty-fifth. Sixty-fifth. Because I was retiring and everyone said I got my freedom. Year last November.

THORN: That was last year?

PETER: Some freedom.

THORN: It can't have been last year if you're seventy-six now, can it?

PETER: Best not ask too many questions, son.

THORN: Son – I'm not your son.

PETER: Do you know that?

THORN: What are you saying, Peter?

PETER: I'm saying I'm off today with a nephew in Brisbane I never knew I had.

THORN: That's life, Peter.

PETER: I haven't got any brothers or sisters. Where's the Jack Rabbit?

THORN: Moored up.

PETER: When d'y last see her?

THORN: I've been so busy with the wedding and all.

PETER: How d'y know she's still there? If you haven't seen her.

THORN: If you're going to start on about fridges lighting up and trees falling down in forests –

PETER: I'm not talking about fridges, Thorn, I'm talking about you and me. What do we really know?

THORN: I know I'm Thorn.

PETER: Says who?

THORN: Some things just are.

PETER: Ours is not to reason why –

THORN: Like me and Noleen.

PETER: Why are you marrying her?

THORN: Because I've always been going to marry Noleen.

PETER: Even though the two of you never talk about anything except your wedding?

THORN: What me and Noleen do and don't talk about is none of your business.

PETER: Even though you haven't had any time alone since Christmas nineteen ninety-three?

THORN: Butt out, Peter.

PETER: You've spent the whole of your engagement standing either side of the counter at Bunny's with half the bay watching you.

THORN: Everyone's been waiting for this wedding for so long.

PETER: What about when the wedding's over?

THORN: We'll have the photos.

PETER: What sort of a life is that?

THORN: We've been engaged for twelve years.

PETER: Maybe you've waited so long you've forgotten what you're waiting for.

THORN: It's such a highlight.

PETER: Like the bus that takes so long to arrive you can't remember where you were going.

THORN: Everyone's bought their outfits.

We start to hear NOLEEN and BUNNY.

PETER: Or even if you want to go there.

THORN: Course I want to go there.

PETER: Do you want to go there, Thorn?

THORN: I was going to give you these.

He gives PETER the wedding rings.

The rings for the wedding.

PETER: I better not.
What if I don't make it back?

THORN: Course you're going to make it back.

PETER: That's how it all starts – one little trip to Brizzie.

THORN: And it turns out you've got a nephew over there?

PETER: Yeah, Barry or something.

THORN: You are the best man, Peter.

He holds them out to PETER.

PETER: If you want me back. I thought maybe you'd changed your mind.

THORN: Day after tomorrow.

PETER: Thanks, Thorn.

THORN: What's all this?

PETER: My clothes.
Gardening stuff.

THORN: It's a lot for an overnight trip.

PETER: Bunny packed it.

THORN: You really need the rake?

BUNNY enters.

BUNNY: Bus is here.

BUNNY starts to collect things from him to pack into the car.

THORN: And the packs of seeds.

PETER: Bunny's keen I take everything. Just in case.

BUNNY exits.

PETER: There's something I want you to know.

BUNNY and NOLEEN are approaching again.

BUNNY: (*Off.*) Give me a hand with this, Nols.

THORN: Go on.

PETER: The world doesn't finish at the end of the bay, you
know.

*NOLEEN and BUNNY enter and carry off PETER's
favourite armchair.*

NOLEEN: It's time to go, Granddad –

They exit.

PETER: Have you ever been in the cabin of the Jack
Rabbit?

THORN: No. I've never thought to go in the cabin.

PETER: If ever things get too much –

BUNNY and NOLEEN enter again to pull PETER off stage.

BUNNY: Let's get him on the bus.

THORN: What about the rest of his stuff?

BUNNY: I'll deal with that later.

They pull him off.

Peter: (*Off.*) If ever things get too much, try the cabin.

THORN is left alone. He looks where PETER has gone, then waves, then turns and picks up PETER's rake and seeds. Looks at them.

Scene Three

Music for the British soap, Arthur Street. *Here we don't see people presenting themselves. We see real people – not aware of the camera. JOELY – huddled against the cold – walks across. We see JOHN walk on – pause to pull his coat collar up around his neck – and walk, across, head down. FLOSS walks across with her trolley. MARY walks across slowly carrying two plastic bags of shopping, her handbag on her shoulder. LORNA comes out to behind the bar of the pub and hands a drink to FLOSS. They never break the realism of their context. Where the Aussie people look happy and relaxed, the British ones look stressed.*

Scene Four

The Duke's. LORNA is getting ready to open up. The post comes through the door, including a letter from America. LORNA gets the post and leafs through it.

She looks at the letter from America. She opens it and starts to read. JOELY enters from outside.

JOELY: What are you doing?

LORNA: This just arrived.

JOELY: Why are you opening my post?

LORNA: It's from America.

JOELY: What right have you got?

LORNA: Is it yours?

JOELY: Give it to me.

LORNA: It's about getting the results of a DNA test.

JOELY: I know what it is.

LORNA: It says they're going to ring you. What's going on, Joely?

JOELY: What do you think?

LORNA: You know who your parents are.

JOELY: I know what you said.

LORNA: Why won't you tell me anything?

JOELY: Like mother like daughter.

LORNA: Talk to me.

JOELY: I came in here to talk to you.

LORNA: We've never rowed like this – not even when there was the fire.

JOELY: I came round to talk. I can't even trust you not to open my post.

LORNA: I'm opening your post because I don't know what's happening and I'm worried about you. What's John doing here?

JOELY: Work it out.

LORNA: John's never denied being your father.

JOELY: That's convenient, isn't it?

LORNA: He's just not been that interested.

JOELY: Convenient for you.

LORNA: I wouldn't call a man who walks out on you six months after you've had his child convenient.

JOELY starts to leave – as FLOSS arrives.

Joely don't go.
John's your father. He was the only man I slept with.
There wasn't anyone else.

FLOSS: What's going on?

JOELY: I don't know you.

LORNA: Of course you know me.

JOELY: I don't know anything about you.

FLOSS: Dear dear.

LORNA: You know me better than anyone.

JOELY: You're not who I thought you were.

LORNA: I am. I haven't changed.

FLOSS tuts.

(*To FLOSS and JOELY.*) How have I changed?

JOELY takes the letter from LORNA.

JOELY: I'll let you know.

She exits to the street. LORNA looks after her. FLOSS picks up the bottle of Australian beer from the bar. She's seen one of these before – she looks at it with nostalgia, then:

FLOSS: Where did you get this?

LORNA looks guilty.

Scene Five

Crystal Bay. BUNNY and NOLEEN are walking along the beach.

BUNNY: Bloody boat.
I don't care what it takes – the wedding's going to be at Bunny's.

NOLEEN: He hadn't mentioned it before.

BUNNY: A wedding's not just about two people. You may love him, but he needs a firm hand – the ideas he gets in his head. A steadying hand. And until you learn to do that for yourself, I'll do it for you.
Like your Granddad sitting pretty in his big house while Thorn moves in with you and me. Flamin' criminal.

NOLEEN: We can't afford a big place like his, Mum.

BUNNY: Exactly.

NOLEEN: Thorn'll sort it, Mum.

BUNNY: Men don't sort anything, you great gallah.
They're like dogs – sniffing along the gutter, never lifting their wet noses to look what's on the horizon. Find some bit of crap they like the scent of and they'll stay there sniffing for years.
He understands about the flowers, doesn't he? The scale of them?

NOLEEN: Thorn?

BUNNY: They're the one thing he has to pay for – that and the cars. I want you hitched – no hitches. You've messed around long enough, you and Thorn. Then there'll be kids. You want a loyal, loving husband not some hoon on a boat with an Oedipal complex and no shirts.

NOLEEN: A what?

BUNNY: You've got to lay it out for them, Nols. Show them how it is and how it's going to be. They're all the same. Don't really understand the world. It's all a bit of a mystery to them.

NOLEEN: It's a bit of a mystery to me.

BUNNY: You'll learn. Couple of ankle biters and a few tonne of dirty laundry you'll get the picture. Thorn just needs a bit of a shove. Bit of a tug on his old lead.

NOLEEN: What sort of a shove?

BUNNY: Don't you worry about that, sweetheart. For the time being, let's leave it that I do the shoving and you do the loving.

Scene Six

Arthur Street, The Duke's. JOHN and JOELY sit at a table.

JOELY: Why did you leave?

JOHN: Sometimes in life, you find yourself doing something and you don't know why you're doing it.

JOELY: No-one wanted you to leave.

JOHN: At the time it felt like I had to.

JOELY: What was Newcastle like?

JOHN: Can't really remember much about it.

JOELY: How old are Karen and Kier?

JOHN: How old?

JOELY: The twins.

JOHN: Karen's twelve and Kevin's eight. Both of them. Eight.

JOELY: Kevin?

JOHN tries to cover up getting his own son's name wrong.

JOHN: Kevin's a nickname. Kevin. Kev. Kier.

JOELY: Didn't you love me?

JOHN: I've always loved you.
Kept a picture of you in my glove compartment.

Sometimes when I was driving I'd pull onto the hard
shoulder, put my hazards on and have a look at it.

JOELY: Really?

JOHN: That's true.

JOELY: Why did you come back?

JOHN: Seems like I can't keep away.
Seems like all roads lead here, for me.

JOELY: I need to know.

JOHN: I need to know too.
Not long now.

JOELY: One phone call'll change everything.

JOHN: Nah. Come on.

They start to leave.

JOELY: You understand, don't you?

JOHN: I understand, Princess.

*JOHN and JOELY are leaving. LORNA and ANNABEL
are behind the bar.*

ANNABEL: They're getting on well.
They must have a lot to say to each other after all these
years.

LORNA: You think so?

ANNABEL: Haven't you got anything to say to him?

LORNA: Why did you walk out and leave me with a pub
and a six-month-old baby.

ANNABEL: Least he didn't leave you with nothing.
That's the last packet of cheese and onion.

LORNA: I'll get some from the cellar.

LORNA slips her coat on and exits into the cellar. As soon as she's gone, ANNABEL starts to rifle through LORNA's bag, which she gets out from under the bar. CHRIS enters.

CHRIS: That's Lorna's bag.

ANNABEL: I'm not stupid.

CHRIS: Nor am I.

ANNABEL: Wouldn't you like to know if your lover was having an affair?
Hold on a minute and we might find out.

CHRIS: What are you on about?

ANNABEL: My bloke and your woman: Mal and Lorna.

CHRIS: She wouldn't –

ANNABEL: Why else d'you think I came to work in this dump?

ANNABEL hasn't found anything.

You want to keep an eye on her.

ANNABEL pulls a pint.

Any fancy clothes. Or jewellery. Weekends away. Mal's got style. What do you think I'm going to do when I find out?
You want a drink?

CHRIS: Yeah.

ANNABEL: Pint?

ANNABEL puts his pint on the table and smiles.

CHRIS: Yeah.

She exits, collecting glasses. CHRIS looks very worried.

Scene Seven

Bunny's. Wedding preparations are well underway. RON is drilling up bunting held by NOLEEN – who is offstage – to BUNNY's orders. THORN is making buttonholes.

RON: I don't know, Bunny.

BUNNY: You just have to give them the rings.

RON: How do I know when?

BUNNY: Noleen says: I –

NOLEEN: (*Off.*) I, Noleen Timpany Delarne –

BUNNY: Take you –

NOLEEN: Take you –

RON: Here all right?

BUNNY: Above the counter, I said.
    Take you –

NOLEEN: (*Off.*) Take you Thorn –

BUNNY: Thorn what?

NOLEEN: Thorn what?

THORN: It's just Thorn.

BUNNY: Course it's not just Thorn.
    What's your other name?

THORN: I don't know.

BUNNY: Nearer the till. Much nearer the till.
    What was your Mother's name?

THORN: Parma.

RON: Like the ham.

THORN: Like the violets.

BUNNY: Parma what?

NOLEEN enters from outside, with the end of the bunting.

THORN: Just Parma.

BUNNY: It's not going to reach if you put it there.

RON: Course it'll reach.

BUNNY: You don't even know where the other end's going.

The phone rings – BUNNY goes to answer it.

NOLEEN: No-one's called just Parma.

We hear bits of BUNNY on the phone under NOLEEN and THORN.

BUNNY: Bunny's. Yes, speaking.

THORN: I need to talk to you.

BUNNY: Hello Dad. How are you?

NOLEEN: About the wedding?

THORN: After the wedding.

NOLEEN: The honeymoon.

BUNNY: What?

THORN: About getting away.

NOLEEN: To Bali.

THORN: On the Jack Rabbit.

NOLEEN: But we're going to Bali, Thorn.

THORN: Getting right away from it all.

NOLEEN: It's all arranged.

BUNNY: What do you mean?

THORN: Before it's too late.

NOLEEN: Mum's picked the tickets up.

THORN: Whose wedding is this, Noleen?

NOLEEN: It's ours.

THORN: Yours or ours?

NOLEEN: Ours.

BUNNY: Oh. Right.

THORN: Your guest list, your honeymoon, your dress, your cake, your rings, your bloody mother.

NOLEEN: Don't call my mother bloody.

LORNA enters.

BUNNY: Of course.

THORN: People live like they're in a box.

NOLEEN: You take that back about her.

THORN: Like the world ends at the edge of the sea and the edge of town.

LORNA sits at a table – maybe with her back to THORN, but close to him. She listens.

All my life I've been here. All my life.

BUNNY: Sure she is.

THORN: Don't you ever wonder what's out there, Nol? What's past the sea?

BUNNY: Hang on a minute.

THORN: Past everything we know?

BUNNY: Noleen?

BUNNY holds the phone out to NOLEEN.

It's Granddad.

THORN: Will you come with me?

NOLEEN walks away from THORN, to the phone. She speaks to PETER.

NOLEEN: (*On the phone.*) Hiya Granddad. Where are you?

LORNA: I'll come with you.

THORN looks at her – amazed.

NOLEEN: (*On the phone.*) Is he? Yeah?

LORNA: Anywhere. Just / away from here.

THORN: Away from here.

NOLEEN: (*On the phone.*) Why not? The wedding's on Friday.

LORNA: Somewhere I know who I am.

Lights up in Arthur Street. CHRIS sits in the Duke's with FLOSS and about eight empty pint glasses around him on the bar – he nurses a ninth.

NOLEEN: (*On the phone.*) Right.

THORN: What if this isn't all there is?

FLOSS: Haven't you had enough?

LORNA: What if the world doesn't end at the end of the street and the end of the bay?

CHRIS: Lorna!

LORNA thinks she hears CHRIS – she's the only one who does.

NOLEEN: (*On the phone.*) Yeah.

CHRIS: Lorna!

LORNA: I have to go.

NOLEEN: (*On the phone.*) See you later, Granddad.

*LORNA runs out of Bunny's, back to the Jack Rabbit.
NOLEEN puts the phone down.*

Mum!
Granddad's staying in Brisbane.

NOLEEN bursts into tears and runs off – behind the counter.

THORN: Peter?

BUNNY: He's tired himself out.
He's eighty-two. He deserves the rest.

THORN: He's sixty-seven.

BUNNY: He's my father. I should know how old he is.

THORN: Eighty-two?

BUNNY: Doesn't sound like he'll be back for the wedding
anyways.

THORN: He'll be back.

BUNNY: You reckon?

*BUNNY looks at THORN, THORN looks into the middle
distance – pensive. We hold the image for a long time, until:
LORNA arrives in the Duke's, out of breath, from Australia.*

FLOSS: Where've you been?

LORNA: In the cellar.

FLOSS: There is no cellar.

ANNABEL enters, with empties.

LORNA: I went to get some more cheese and onion crisps.

ANNABEL: So where are they?

FLOSS: Where've you been?

CHRIS: You can't do this to me Lorna – go and get crisps
and not get any – who's Joely's father?

LORNA: John –

ANNABEL: You sure about that?

CHRIS: Where've you been?

ANNABEL: Same again, Chris?

LORNA: What's going on? What's happening to us, Chris?

CHRIS: You tell me.

ANNABEL puts another pint on the bar for CHRIS.

FLOSS: I'll tell you.

LORNA: You don't normally shout like this. And drinking in the day.

FLOSS: He's become an alcoholic.

CHRIS: Are you having an affair?

LORNA: No.

LORNA takes her coat off. Underneath is a tacky posh bejewelled off-the-shoulder dress. Everyone stares at it. No-one is more surprised than LORNA. CHRIS stands up violently.

FLOSS: He's getting violent and out of control.

ANNABEL: I knew it.

FLOSS: No good will come of it.

LORNA: Of what?

FLOSS: Drink, violence, new barmaid, DNA test.

CHRIS: I've had enough.

LORNA: What have I done?

CHRIS gets up.

CHRIS: You've betrayed me.

CHRIS storms out.

ANNABEL: You won't get away with this, Lorna.

LORNA starts to exit to the cellar.

LORNA: I forgot the crisps –

FLOSS: It's stacking up against you, Lorna.

LORNA exits to the cellar. As she opens the door, the bright sunshine of Australia and the sound of the sea floods through.

Scene Eight

The sounds of the sea from the previous scene swell to reveal LISA on the beach, looking out to sea. Her hair blows. NEALE enters, comes up behind her and stands. She doesn't look round. They don't touch.

LISA: When the tide's coming in this quick, you think it'll never stop.

NEALE: It always does, but.

LISA: Just for a moment you think it'll keep on going. Wash everything away.

NEALE: When I was in Remand, all I wanted to do was get home.
But Crystal Bay isn't my home.

LISA: It is home.

NEALE: When I'm with you, I'm home.

He goes to touch her. LORNA appears out of the cabin of the Jack Rabbit, and runs across the back of the scene in her spangly dress, racing to find THORN. The others don't notice her.

LISA: I can't do this.

NEALE: How can we not do it?

LISA: Thorn's my anchor. If he lets go of me, I'll just drift away.

They are both distraught.

Scene Nine

SHARP's bedroom. ANNABEL is rifling through SHARP's drawers and bed, looking for evidence of LORNA.

ANNABEL: I know you've been here.
I know you have.
I'll find you.
You don't do this to me.
Where are you?
Where are you, Lorna Bates?

She exits, with evil in her eyes.

Scene Ten

Bunny's Café. BUNNY is at the counter. THORN enters with his suit.

BUNNY: You got it –

THORN: I've been thinking –

BUNNY: I was about to send a search party out.

THORN: About Peter.

BUNNY: What about him?

THORN: If he can't make the wedding, we should have it on the Jack Rabbit, in his honour.

BUNNY: I don't think so.

THORN: What about what I think?

BUNNY: This isn't just about you, Thorn.

THORN: Who's getting married, Bunny?

BUNNY: My daughter. I'd like to know she meant more to you than that outsized dinghy.

THORN: Of course she does.

BUNNY: Prove it.

THORN: I'm not having this conversation, Bunny.

BUNNY: Prove it by having the wedding here –

THORN: Get your face out –

BUNNY: And forgetting about that fish-stinker.

THORN: Get your face out of my life, Bunny.

BUNNY: There's nothing I'd like better.

NOLEEN enters from the kitchen.

Hiya, sweetheart.

THORN: Nols –

NOLEEN: Let's see it.

THORN: What?

BUNNY: The suit.

NOLEEN: Why don't you put it on?

THORN: I don't think I will right now.

BUNNY: You really should try it on, Thorn.

THORN takes his jacket off and puts his wedding suit jacket on.

We don't want to make any mistakes.

THORN: It's great.

He starts to take it off again.

NOLEEN: You haven't done the buttons up.

She pulls it back on and does the buttons up.

BUNNY: We don't want anything to ruin the big day.

THORN: It's perfect.

NOLEEN: And the strides.

He puts the trousers on.

BUNNY: What d'y reckon, Noleen?

NOLEEN smiles.

Give us a twirl.

He turns round reluctantly. LORNA enters through the café door.

We're closed.

THORN and LORNA look at each other.

What do you want?

THORN: This is –

LORNA: Lorna.

BUNNY and NOLEEN are puzzled – this isn't what they were expecting. It feels like the storyline's really creaking.

NOLEEN: Lorna?

THORN: From the bridal wear shop. They were worried the sleeves are too long.

NOLEEN: It's made-to-measure.

BUNNY: They were too short last time.

LORNA: That's sleeves for you.

LORNA starts to turn the sleeves under a bit – but she has no pins or anything.

What do you think?

The others still gape at her.

BUNNY: Didn't you bring any pins?

LORNA: I like to do things by eye.

BUNNY: They look fine to me.

NOLEEN: I think they're perfect.

LORNA: (*To THORN.*) I think I'm going to die.

BUNNY: We don't want them too short, he'll look like a crim.

LORNA: (*To THORN.*) A long way away from here. They're killing me.

NOLEEN: But if they're too long, no-one'll be able to see the ring.

LORNA: (*To THORN.*) Everything about me's changing.

(*To NOLEEN and BUNNY.*) How's that?

NOLEEN: Too / long –

BUNNY: Too / short.

As LORNA and THORN continue, BUNNY and NOLEEN argue about the length of the sleeves.

LORNA: (*To THORN.*) I don't know whose these clothes are.

BUNNY: They can't be too long, sweetheart – she's turning them up and they weren't too long in the first place.

THORN: (*To LORNA.*) I don't want to marry Noleen.

BUNNY: (*To LORNA.*) Turn them down a bit.

NOLEEN: No!

LORNA: (*To THORN.*) I have to get away.

BUNNY: Trust me, Noleen.

THORN: (*To LORNA.*) I've got a boat.

LORNA: (*To THORN.*) The Jack Rabbit.

NOLEEN: I want everything to be right.

THORN: (*To LORNA.*) When?

BUNNY: It will be right.

LORNA: (*To THORN.*) I have to talk to my daughter.

THORN: (*To LORNA.*) You've got a daughter?

NOLEEN: I've got a funny feeling it won't.

LORNA: (*To THORN.*) She's sixteen.

THORN: (*To LORNA.*) Same age as my sister.

NOLEEN: I've got a really funny feeling.

LORNA: (*To THORN.*) I was very young.

THORN: (*To LORNA.*) Tonight?

BUNNY: Just relax, darl. Leave it all to me.

LORNA: (*To THORN.*) Seven o'clock tonight.

NOLEEN: You work at Lace and Dreams?

THORN nods discreetly.

LORNA: Yes.

NOLEEN: I've never seen you there, but.

LORNA: I only do grooms, not bridal.
Well I think that's going to be fine.

LORNA starts to leave.

I'd better go.

BUNNY: Aren't you going to take the suit with you?

LORNA: I could get it later.

NOLEEN: We're getting married the day after tomorrow.

THORN has to strip off in front of her. She tries to avert her eyes and take the suit without looking at him – but at the last moment she looks. Their eyes meet.

How long will it take?

BUNNY: I want that suit back here by midday tomorrow. Clean, pressed and ready to go.

THORN and LORNA's eyes are locked.

That doesn't give you long. You know that, don't you?

LORNA and THORN still look at each other.

LORNA: I'll be as quick as I can.

LORNA runs out with the suit. THORN puts his clothes back on.

BUNNY: Where are you going?

THORN: I've got things to do.

NOLEEN: Thorn?

BUNNY: On the Jack Rabbit?

THORN: Nah.

BUNNY: Nah?

THORN: Nah.

They look at each other, then THORN exits. NOLEEN looks after him, lovingly. BUNNY looks secretly delighted.

Scene Eleven

Outside MARY's back door. JOELY comes out. LORNA enters, still holding THORN's suit.

LORNA: Joely –

JOELY: I don't want to speak to you –

LORNA: I'm leaving.

JOELY: You're running away.

LORNA: I've got to get out. Before it's too late. Will you come with me?

JOELY: You know I won't.

LORNA: John is your Dad.

JOELY: How can I believe you?

LORNA: I didn't sleep with anyone else.

JOELY: How do I know you're telling me the truth?

LORNA: Because I've never lied to you.

JOELY: Why have you got that suit?

LORNA: I'm looking after it for a friend.

JOELY: What friend?

LORNA can't explain.

Why should I believe you over everyone else?

LORNA: I'm the person who loves you most in the world.

JOELY: Even if I have to stop believing in the rest of the world?

LORNA: You have to choose what you believe, Joely.
I haven't changed.

JOELY: So why do I feel I don't know you any more?

LORNA: Things are changing around us.
You'll know what I'm talking about when it happens to you.

JOELY: I have to meet Dad in the Duke's.

LORNA: And when it does, you bang on the cellar door and I'll be there for you.

The two women look at each other. JOELY leaves.

Scene Twelve

Bunny's. BUNNY comes out from the kitchen with a big sharp knife that glints in the light. She calls back to NOLEEN.

BUNNY: Noleen? I'm just popping out for an hour.

She exits to the bay, smiling to herself.

Scene Thirteen

The beach. NEALE and LISA still stand, looking out to sea.

LISA: I'm just Thorn's little sister. That's all I am.

NEALE: You're more than that.

LISA: Thorn's the only one who ever really talks to me – usually about Mum and Dad, or about Noleen. He's the only one.

NEALE: I'm here now.

LISA: Thorn's always been there for me. Nobody else knows anything about me.

NEALE: I do.

LISA: No you don't. I don't. All I really know is my name. Talking to you these last few days is the most I've ever said to anyone.

NEALE: So keep talking.

LISA: Quite often I'm around, sitting at a table in Bunny's, or lying on the beach – but it's like I'm not there, like no-one can see me.

NEALE: I can see you.

LISA: Can you?

NEALE: You're all I can see.

They kiss, passionately.

71

Scene Fourteen

The Duke's. MARY sits at a table. FLOSS is at the bar, ANNABEL behind it. JOHN is getting a round in at the bar.

ANNABEL: What're you staring at?

FLOSS: Dunno, the label's fallen off.

ANNABEL: I haven't got a label.

FLOSS: We've all got labels.

JOHN arrives at the bar.

ANNABEL: Try Goddess.

CHRIS enters, drunk. He's holding a nearly empty bottle of whisky.

JOHN: Chris?

CHRIS: What about it?

JOHN: John Dove.

CHRIS: I know who you are.
You getting the drinks in?

JOHN: Don't you think you've had enough?

CHRIS: Enough of being messed about and taken for a ride.

JOHN goes over to MARY's table with the drinks. JOELY enters and joins them, puts her mobile phone on the table.

JOHN: Cheers.

They all clink glasses.

MARY: You don't know what this means to me.

JOHN: I know what it means to you, Mum.

JOELY gets the American letter out, she looks at it.

MARY: All these feet under the table and mouths to feed.

JOHN: I know Mum. All right, love?

JOELY: It says they'll ring before eight.

MARY: I have plenty of guests at the B and B.

JOHN: I know you do, Mum.

MARY: Some of them stay years.

JOHN looks at his watch.

JOHN: Few minutes yet.

MARY: But even when they have bed and breakfast and the evening meal, it ain't the same as having family.

JOHN: All right, Mum.

MARY: It's family.

JOHN: Don't press the family button too hard, Mum.

JOELY's mobile rings. All eyes on JOELY. JOELY looks at JOHN.

You want me to answer it?

JOELY: No.

She picks up the phone.

Hello?
Speaking.
Yes.
Yes – my Nan and – and my Dad.
So what does that mean?
What does that mean?
No.
I understand.
Yes.
Yes I will.
Thank-you.

'Bye.

She hangs up. She shakes her head.

You're not my father.

MARY: You sure?

JOHN: That's what she said, isn't it?

JOELY looks at the table.

ANNABEL: No surprise – given Lorna's current record.

JOHN: I'm not your father.

ANNABEL: Can I get you a drink, Chris?

CHRIS nods and hands her a glass.

CHRIS: I don't ever want to see her again.

MARY: That means I'm not your Nan.

JOHN: You all right, Joely?

CHRIS addresses the pub.

CHRIS: That's all of us, isn't it?

FLOSS: Looks like we're in for a storm.

MARY: All these years.

CHRIS: She's been having us all on.

Thunder and lightning crack and flash.

Scene Fifteen

The Jack Rabbit. THORN and LORNA stand on the deck. LORNA has THORN's wedding suit.

THORN: We'll have to wait for this to die down. We can't risk it.

LORNA: What if someone finds us?

THORN: No-one'll find us here.

LORNA: I brought you this.

She gives him the suit.

I don't know if you still need it.

THORN: No.

He hangs it up or puts it down. The boat rocks a bit.

All right?

LORNA: I will be once we get away.
Is this a sailing boat?

THORN: I think so.

LORNA: Has it got sails?

THORN: Yes it has.

LORNA: So it's a sailing boat?

THORN: Yes – it's a sailing boat, it's a sailing boat!

LORNA: Can you sail it?

THORN: It's my job – I take people out on it every day.
But you know – I have absolutely no memory of any of
it.

*The boat lurches and the cabin door opens, out come some
half-burnt wrapped Christmas presents and a black curly-
permed wig. LORNA picks up the wig.*

LORNA: This is my hair from nineteen eighty-six.

THORN: I don't know myself.

LORNA picks up a half-burnt, wrapped Christmas present.

LORNA: Oh.

THORN: My most distinguishing features, the things I
thought meant the most to me are just skin deep.

LORNA: There was a fire at the pub. 1994. I left the gas on.

LORNA picks out more half-burnt, wrapped Christmas presents.

THORN: Everything I've achieved up to this point in my life has been meaningless trivia.

LORNA: I had to get out with Joely. She was only five – six. It was Christmas and all our presents – these were all our presents.

The boat rocks again and the cabin door flies open and this time out comes PETER, holding a ring box.

THORN: Peter.

PETER: You don't know how pleased I am to see you.

THORN: How did you get here?

PETER: Dunno, mate. One minute I was on the bus to Brizzie and the next –

LORNA: Have you been to the pub?

PETER: Not a chance – bus just keeps on going.

THORN: This is Lorna.

PETER: Lorna.

LORNA smiles.

THORN: Those my rings?

PETER opens the box. He's surprised by what's inside.

PETER: No, mate.
This one's mine.

THORN: Only there's been a change of plan. We're going away on the Jack Rabbit. Once this storm's passed.

PETER looks at the ring.

PETER: I've spent my life dreaming of getting away on the Jack Rabbit.

LORNA: So what do we do?

THORN: We can't go anywhere in this weather.

PETER: We'll have to wait for this storm to pass.

THORN: It'll pass in a minute.

PETER: It's me. I'm bad luck. I should get off.

THORN: Storms don't last long here.

PETER: I really loved her.

THORN: Who?

PETER: I never meant to have an affair, but I was married to someone I never got to know.

THORN: Your wife.

PETER: My wife and me – we hardly saw each other. I didn't know what love was. Until I met this girl. We were going to go away. On the Jack Rabbit.
I waited and waited and she never came. Camped out on the boat waiting for weeks, months. And then one day the cabin door opened and this little bundle came through. A baby. Our baby.

THORN: Bunny.

PETER: And I knew then it was over. Came ashore. What else could I do? I had a little girl to look after. It happens. Babies appear. Kids you never knew you had. No-one batted an eyelid. Not even my wife.

LORNA: You still love her.

PETER: Part of me'll always be waiting for her.

He looks at the ring in its box.

I bought her this when my wife died so tragically.
Thought if I ever saw her –

*Another big lurch and a tombstone comes out from the cabin
– they all fall backwards, THORN catching the tombstone
like a rugby ball – it winds him. As PETER talks, THORN
looks at it.*

LORNA: What?

PETER: You don't want to see this.

She looks.

LORNA: It's mine –

*THORN goes to throw it off the boat. LORNA grabs hold of it
and looks again.*

May the eleventh nineteen seventy-four to (date of
performance).

THORN throws it overboard – splash.

THORN: We've got to go.

PETER: We don't stand a chance in this.

THORN: Lorna doesn't stand a chance if we don't.

PETER: Wait for the wind to change. We can't cast off in
this.

The boat lurches.

THORN: What was that?

LORNA: Thorn?

*Another lurch – they all fall to the ground and the end of a
rope flicks up onto the deck, soaking wet.*

THORN: That's the mooring rope.

THORN grabs the end of the rope.

PETER: It must have snapped.

THORN: You know how to sail the boat, don't you mate?

As they try to get control of the boat, they're being thrown around.

PETER: I should do –

THORN: Me too –

PETER: Isn't there something about a for'd and a stern?

THORN: For'd and aft.

PETER: And a mainsail.

THORN: And the Jib and the forestay –

LORNA: What's happening?

PETER: And the shrouds.

THORN: And the pulpit.

PETER: And the pushpit.

They are being thrown around on the boat.

LORNA: Do something!

THORN: We have to turn her –

We hear NOLEEN and BUNNY from the shore.

NOLEEN: (*Off.*) The Jack Rabbit!

PETER: Get the sails up.

NOLEEN: (*Off.*) Mum!

THORN raises the sail. PETER's trying to start the engine.

PETER: It won't start. I'm not getting anything.

BUNNY: (*Off.*) Noleen!

THORN: We'll never get head to wind.

NOLEEN: (*Off.*) There's someone on deck!

BUNNY: (*Off.*) No!

THORN: She's too close to the rocks –

They start trying to sail, but are being chucked around.

NOLEEN: (*Off.*) Ron –

BUNNY: (*Off.*) It's Thorn –

PETER: The blocks have jammed.

NOLEEN: (*Off.*) Thorn!

THORN: I can't get any steerage –

BUNNY: (*Off.*) Ron!

THORN: I can't turn her.

BUNNY: (*Off.*) Noleen, come away!

RON: (*Off.*) Thorn!

BUNNY: (*Off.*) Be careful, Ron!

RON: (*Off.*) Thorn!

PETER: It's broaching – it's broaching –

BUNNY: (*Off.*) Noleen, come away!

THORN: Lee shore! Lee shore!

A big lurch and LORNA gets thrown back into the cabin.

LORNA: Thorn!

A crash of thunder and flash of lightning.

THORN: Lorna!!

The crash of the boat hitting the rocks. And we're in darkness.

Episode 3: Friday

Scene One

The theme tune for Crystal Bay. *Credits begin, but as they continue, we see moments from the UK soap and bits of its music infiltrate too. Settings are also changed: some of the UK action we see against the Aussie setting, and sometimes the Aussie vignettes take place in the UK settings.*

NOLEEN runs on, but there is no THORN. She stops, looks around for him. She runs off again.

PETER with a spade. He is about to dig, then stops. Looks up – he's seen someone. He salutes them and laughs. They go. He wipes his brow and cocks his head to one side. All's right with the world.

JOELY – huddled against the cold – walks across.

NEALE – whittling a piece of wood with a knife – he looks up, moody.

MARY walks across slowly carrying two plastic bags of shopping, her handbag on her shoulder.

We see JOHN walk on – pause to pull his coat collar up around his neck – and walk across, head down.

BUNNY walks on with a coffee in one hand and a piece of cake on a plate in the other. She catches an unseen customer's eye and walks, as if over to them holding out their order.

We see CHRIS weave drunkenly across the space.

RON – about to drill something. He turns his head – pauses – and looks into the middle distance.

FLOSS walks across with her trolley.

LISA comes on, blown by the wind. She smiles, looking into the middle distance.

ANNABEL comes out to behind the bar of the pub and hands a drink to FLOSS.

Scene 2

MARY's back door. JOHN is coming out with his suitcase – he's leaving. MARY comes after him.

MARY: Fifteen years you haven't set foot round here. Fifteen years Lorna's brought up Joely, cared for her. We haven't heard a squeak out of you.

JOHN: Squeak, squeak.

MARY: Not a squeak.

JOHN: I send birthday cards and Christmas, Mother's Day cards.

MARY: What's a card? Picture of roses or a horse and carriage in the snow and some bit of verse you haven't even read before you put your name to it? Mother's Day card always arrives on Monday.

JOHN: Not fair, is it Mum?

MARY: I haven't had one on the Sunday yet.

JOHN: No point sitting here waiting for it to get fair – you'll be here all your life.

MARY: I've been here all my life.

JOHN: Hasn't changed much, has it? Just new paper on your walls.

MARY: Nothing to do with me.

JOHN: Someone's decorated for you.

MARY: I came home and there was a new sofa, new wallpaper. When I looked in the mirror I had old woman's hair. That's who I am. Just the Bed and Breakfast woman. I used to be someone's mother, but no-one remembers that.

JOHN: I remember, mum.

MARY: I was a good mother to you.

JOHN: You were.

MARY: I still am. Trying to hold my family together. All I wanted was my family around me and happy. And I've failed. Always failed.

JOHN: I'm here now, aren't I?

MARY: You've got a whole new life. Grandchildren I've never met – my only grandchildren.
Why did you leave me?

JOHN: Who knows why we do what we do?

MARY: Mopped the same square of lino for forty years. Why can't we all be a family, together?

JOHN: There is no family. It's in the DNA.

MARY: I've nearly killed myself for my family, and now I haven't got one.

JOHN: Let me go, Mum.

MARY: If I have no family, who have I done all this for?

JOHN picks up his case.

You're all I've got.

JOHN: You haven't got me.

MARY: You're my son. My child.
John, where are you going?

JOHN: I'll just get in the car and drive, Mum.

MARY: Drive where?

JOHN: Remember the last time?

MARY: June the fourteenth nineteen eighty nine.

JOHN: I drove through the night and through the night and the morning never came and Newcastle never came. Driving through the dark until at last I saw lights. Streetlights and shops and the Duke's and your house and you standing at the door. It'd taken me fifteen years and I'd come home.
All the time I was driving I'd thought I was moving towards something, some dream.

MARY: And you were coming home.

JOHN starts to exit – maybe with his car keys.

JOHN: See you at Christmas, Mum.

She calls after him.

MARY: Which Christmas! John – which Christmas!

JOHN's gone. MARY looks out from her back door.

Scene Three

The hospital, Crystal Bay. THORN lies in a bed, unconscious and wired up to machines.

His head is bandaged. NOLEEN sits next to THORN. She holds his closed hand. In it is a length of rope: the end he's holding has been cut, the other end has a broken fixing on it.

NOLEEN: The vicar's been very kind.
He says there's still a few hours before the service and as long as you're fully conscious by then, he's happy and the wedding can go ahead right here.

She tries to open his hand.

Let go of it, Thorn. Let go.
He's going to come in himself to chat to you spiritually.

She tries to prise the rope out of his hand.

Let go.

He says he's praying for you and asking his
congregation to join him in prayer.
Open your hand, for God's sake.
Everyone's praying for you, Thorn. We all want you to
wake up.
Open it.

*As she pulls at his fingers again, PETER is wheeled in in a
bed, by BUNNY and a NURSE.*

BUNNY: Here we are, Dad. Let me tuck you up.

PETER: I'm all right.

BUNNY: You heard what the Doc said – bed rest.

*The NURSE exits. As they continue, NOLEEN is almost
weeping over THORN's closed fist.*

PETER: What am I doing?

BUNNY: You need specialist care.

PETER: Leave it, love.

NOLEEN: Why won't he hold my hand?

BUNNY: He doesn't know what he's doing, Noleen.

BUNNY exits.

PETER: Don't fret, love.
 I've got some lemon barley on the side, here.

NOLEEN shakes her head.

 You got to eat and drink sometime, love.

*BUNNY and a NURSE enter with RON in a third bed,
wheeling him on.*

 What use are you to him if you're fading away?
 You want to get some shut-eye.

NOLEEN: I can't – not with him just lying there.

BUNNY: Just park you here, Ron. Thank you, nurse.

The NURSE exits.

NOLEEN: What if he doesn't wake up?

PETER: He'll wake-up all right.

NOLEEN: Do you think so, Granddad?

PETER: Sure so, Noleen.

RON: And when he does, who's going to tell him about the Jack Rabbit?

They all look at THORN's hand with the rope in it.

Scene Four

Arthur Street. SHARP's Bedroom. SHARP is in bed – a distinguishing wig peeps out of the covers. There is another figure next to him, also asleep. It is LORNA. She wakes with a start, sitting up in bed. She is soaking wet and still wearing her coat. Her shoes are placed next to the bed, neatly.

LORNA: Thorn?

She looks around – at first she can't work out what's going on – and then she realises she's in a strange man's bedroom.

(*Quiet.*) No!
This isn't me.

SHARP shifts in bed – LORNA freezes, as far away as the bed will allow her to get from him. He settles again. She sees a photograph. She picks it up – it's a picture of SHARP and ANNABEL.

(*Quiet.*) Annabel.

She looks across at SHARP. She carefully gets out of the bed, putting the covers back over him. It is only now that she registers that she's soaking wet – the bed is wet where she's lain. She creeps, dripping, from the room. Her shoes remain next to the bed. Still SHARP sleeps.

Scene Five

The hospital. RON and PETER are dozing. NOLEEN holds THORN's closed hand. THORN starts to come to – as though from a dream. His speech incoherent at first.

THORN: I can't get any steerage –

He thrashes about, trying to get up.

NOLEEN: He's waking up!

THORN: I can't turn her.

NOLEEN: Thorn!

NOLEEN tries to hold him back and hold all his wires in place – the other two men stir and come over.

THORN: Lee shore! Lee shore!

NOLEEN: He's waking up!

THORN: Who are you?

BUNNY: Someone get the Doc.

Nobody does.

THORN: Where is she?

NOLEEN: I'm here.

THORN: The Jack Rabbit.

PETER: It's all over, Thorn.

RON: It's all right, mate.

NOLEEN: I'll get the doctor.

RON: Holy Dooley.

NOLEEN goes.

PETER: Are you all right?

THORN: Peter?

BUNNY: You're in hospital.

PETER: You've had a bit of a bump on your head. Bit of a nasty one. That's all.

THORN: You're in your pyjamas, Peter.

RON: We're all in our pyjamas, Thorn. Nothing for you to worry yourself about.

NOLEEN comes in.

NOLEEN: Doctor's coming.

She goes over to THORN.

You've woken up.

THORN: Who are you?

NOLEEN: Noleen.

BUNNY: Your fiancée.

NOLEEN: Doesn't he remember me?

BUNNY: Course he remembers you.

RON: You remember Noleen, don't you Thorn?

THORN: And flowers.

NOLEEN: Yes – we went to look at flowers for the wedding.

THORN: The wedding.

BUNNY: The wedding.

THORN: The Jack Rabbit.

RON: He keeps on about the Jack Rabbit.

BUNNY: Does he know what happened?

RON: Hasn't got the foggiest.

NOLEEN: Do you think he's all right?

RON: He's all right.

THORN: Where is she?

NOLEEN: I'm here, Thorn.

THORN: Lee shore! Lee shore!

BUNNY: What's he on about?

THORN: The Jack Rabbit. I had this terrible dream.

NOLEEN: It wasn't a dream, Thorn.

RON: It's gone, mate.
  The Jack Rabbit's gone.

THORN: Gone?

NOLEEN: I'm going to get the Doc.

  She exits.

PETER: The Jack Rabbit's no more, mate.

  THORN looks at the rope he holds in his hands. Everyone looks at the rope.

  There was a storm. She came loose from her moorings.
  The rope snapped – just gave way.
  We all tried to save her, Thorn. All of us.

THORN: This rope didn't snap. It's been cut.

RON / BUNNY: What?

THORN: It's a clean break.

PETER: He's right.

THORN: Someone severed her from her moorings. Let her out onto the open sea.

RON: With a storm raging.

PETER: Let the sea take her.

THORN: Someone did this.

PETER: But who?

RON: Who would do that, Thorn?

PETER: Who wants rid of the Jack Rabbit?

BUNNY: I saw Neale on the beach last night.

PETER: Neale?

RON: Neale?

THORN: Neale Bolton.

BUNNY: He had something with him that was flashing in the moonlight.

THORN: A knife.

They all look into the middle distance in different directions.

Scene Six

UK. SHARP's bedroom. SHARP has gone. CHRIS enters, drunk. He pulls back the covers on the bed – nobody there.

CHRIS: Where are you?

He starts to look under furniture – trashing the place.

Come on.
You think you can do this to me and I'll just walk away?
Where are you?

ANNABEL enters and tries to stop him.

ANNABEL: Chris –

CHRIS: Get off me –

ANNABEL: This isn't going to do any good.

CHRIS: It's doing me good.

ANNABEL: They're not here.

CHRIS: I want to see it with my own eyes.

ANNABEL: You don't.

CHRIS: I want to know.

ANNABEL: Stop it.

CHRIS: I feel like I'm spinning, like I'm spinning and I just want it to stop.

ANNABEL: Sit down.

CHRIS: I don't mean like that. I mean inside. My life's spinning. I want it to stop. I want to know. I want to know where I stand.

He sits down. He sees LORNA's shoes next to the bed. He picks them up.

ANNABEL: They don't care about us.

CHRIS: I've cleaned these for her before now.

ANNABEL: When they're here together, they're not thinking about us.

CHRIS: She's wrecked everything for me.

ANNABEL: She's wrecked everything for me.

CHRIS: She's smashed it all up.

ANNABEL: She's smashed it up for me.

CHRIS: I wish she was dead.

ANNABEL: I wish she was dead too.

ANNABEL takes the shoes from him and puts them on the floor.

CHRIS: I never thought she'd do something like this.

ANNABEL: You never know what's round the corner.

ANNABEL kisses him. He pulls away.

Let me make it better.

They kiss.

Scene Seven

The hospital. Back to where we left off.

THORN: He did it again.

PETER: Who?

RON: What?

BUNNY: Neale Bolton.

RON: What?

THORN: Couldn't help himself. And this time he nearly succeeded. He nearly killed me.

RON: Streuth.

THORN: That's what this has always been about.

LISA enters. She has a six pack of beer.

LISA: Thorn – you're awake.
Is he okay?

RON: It's all right, Lis, he's not going to kark it.

LISA: We went down to see the Jack Rabbit.

THORN: Who's we?

NEALE enters. He has THORN's drenched wedding suit, still on its hanger.

NEALE: We found this on the beach.

He holds up THORN's suit. THORN addresses NEALE.

THORN: Come to finish me off, have you?

NOLEEN enters.

NOLEEN: What's happening?

LISA: What are you talking about, Thorn?

NOLEEN sees THORN's suit.

NOLEEN: His suit.

NEALE: Look, I'm sorry about before.

NOLEEN: Mum!

BUNNY: It'll sponge all right.

NEALE: All those years ago.

> *THORN starts to get out of bed.*

NOLEEN: Lie down, Thorn.

NEALE: About the school.

> *THORN struggles to get out of bed as everyone tries to keep him in – pasting wires back on as he rips them off and machines fly around.*

RON: Thorn –

LISA: No!

NEALE: The fire.

PETER: He's mad.

NEALE: But it wasn't personal.

> *THORN makes it out of bed and attacks NEALE.*

NOLEEN: Stop him somebody.

NEALE: It wasn't anything to do with you.

THORN: You were seen.

NOLEEN: Stop him.

LISA: He didn't do anything.

NEALE: I've done my time.

THORN: Last night.

NEALE: I know the fire was wrong.

THORN: On the beach.

NEALE: I've changed.

THORN: You had a knife.

NOLEEN: He had a knife?

BUNNY: Yeah.

LISA: He was with me last night.

NEALE: I didn't touch the boat.

THORN: You cut the Jack Rabbit from her moorings.

NOLEEN: Neale?

NEALE: There was a storm.

BUNNY: That's what he wants us to think.

LISA: He was with me at home.

THORN: You destroyed her like you want to destroy me.

NEALE: I didn't touch the Jack Rabbit.

THORN: You wrecked the Jack Rabbit.

BUNNY: Yeah.

NEALE: Let me go.

LISA: Let him go.

THORN: Keep out of this, Lisa.

PETER: Let him go, Thorn.

NOLEEN: Let him go.

They manage to get THORN off NEALE long enough for NEALE to escape. The two men breathe heavily for a while.

NEALE: Lisa?

LISA turns to go with NEALE.

THORN: Lis?

LISA turns away from THORN and goes with NEALE.
THORN swoons.

PETER: Get him on the bed.

NOLEEN: Someone fetch the Doctor.

BUNNY goes as they get him back on his bed.

It's all right sweetheart.
He's gone now.

RON starts to set the machines right.

RON: He won't be coming back in a hurry.

THORN: (*To PETER.*) The Jack Rabbit.

NOLEEN: Is he going to be okay, Ron?

THORN: (*To PETER.*) What happened?

PETER: (*To THORN.*) The storm.

RON: He'll be right, sweets.

NOLEEN: You think so?

PETER: (*To THORN.*) Lorna went back into the cabin.

RON: That doctor coming?

NOLEEN: Mum's gone to fetch him.

THORN: (*To PETER.*) Where's the cabin?

PETER: (*To THORN.*) I don't know.

He puts his dressing gown on.

RON: Perhaps some pills might help.

NOLEEN: Some pills, yeah.

THORN: (*To PETER.*) I have to find her. Find the cabin.

PETER: (*To THORN.*) I'll see what I can do.
(*To RON.*) Just popping to the men's room.

PETER exits.

THORN: Where is she?

NOLEEN: I'm here, Thorn.

BUNNY returns.

BUNNY: Doctor's coming.

RON: Forget about it, Thorn.

BUNNY: Where's Peter.

RON: Just popped to the dunny.

THORN looks blankly at her.

THORN: Do we know each other?

NOLEEN: It's me, Noleen.

THORN: Are we married?

NOLEEN: We're going to be, Thorn.

BUNNY: Just as soon as you get dressed.

THORN: On the Jack Rabbit?

BUNNY: We're not using the boat, Thorn.

NOLEEN: It's all arranged.

THORN: We're getting married?

NOLEEN: Of course we are.

RON gets his tools out from his bedside cabinet.

BUNNY: Right here, Thorn.

THORN: Here?

NOLEEN: Here.

RON: In the crock house?

BUNNY: Leave everything to me, boys.

RON drills a machine. Everyone looks at him.

Scene Eight

The cellar door. LORNA hurries on and tries the door, she can't push it open. She tries some more.

LORNA: Come on. Open! Open!

FLOSS appears behind her, rubber gloves on, holding a duster.

FLOSS: More crisps?

LORNA sees her.

LORNA: Yes.

FLOSS: What flavour this time?
Barbecued kangaroo?

LORNA: No.

FLOSS: Not leaving us, are you?
Not without a big send off.

LORNA: I need to get into the cellar.

FLOSS: When I ran the Duke's there wasn't a cellar.

LORNA: I've had some work done.

FLOSS: What's behind the door?

LORNA: Nothing.

FLOSS: Golden beaches and sparkling waves?

LORNA: Just storage.

FLOSS: The weather might be better, but it's just the same as here.

LORNA: How do you know?

FLOSS: You meet some hunk with a boat and think all your troubles are over.

LORNA: You.

FLOSS: Well they're not.

LORNA: You've been through.

FLOSS: All you get through there is trouble.

LORNA: It was you.

FLOSS: Is that what you want?

LORNA: It was you met Peter.

FLOSS: You're in enough trouble already.

LORNA: I'm not in any trouble.

FLOSS: Spooky barmaid, alcoholic boyfriend, DNA test daughter –

LORNA: John is Joely's father.

FLOSS: People tell you things about yourself, about your own life you've never heard before.

LORNA: I didn't sleep with anyone else.

FLOSS: Maybe they did happen, maybe they didn't happen how you remember.

LORNA: From the moment I had Joely she was all I wanted. For her to be happy. How can I make her happy if the man I slept with isn't her father and I don't know about it? It's not possible.

FLOSS: Maybe it doesn't matter how it happened.

LORNA: I've got a daughter I'm not old enough to have, and we've only had about three birthdays between us. How can I have any self-belief if I am not possible, if my life is not plausible?

FLOSS: Everything you do is plausible – it's just when you put it all together –

LORNA: I'm not interested in being a series of moments.

FLOSS: Moments are all we have.

LORNA: I want continuity.

FLOSS: We all want that. We all want an epic – from birth
to the grave, but this isn't just about you.
If everything was always about you, what would happen
to the rest of us?

LORNA: I don't want to live like this.

FLOSS: Then you don't want to live.

LORNA: Not if it means I end up like you.

FLOSS: I'm still alive.

LORNA: Is the only point of living to stay alive? On the
other side of the world from the person you love – from
your own child.

FLOSS: And you're taking Joely, are you?

LORNA: She's old enough to make up her own mind.

FLOSS: He's not her father, by the way. The DNA results
came through.

FLOSS starts to leave – then turns back.

This is your story, like it or not. It's not *Gone with the
Wind*, it's not *Doctor Zhivago*.

She starts to go again.

Want to know what happens next?

LORNA looks at her in horror.

No – I bet you don't.

*FLOSS leaves, cackling. LORNA turns back to the door and
hammers on it.*

LORNA: Thorn! Thorn!!

Scene Nine

The hospital, Crystal Bay. The wedding is about to start. THORN is sitting up in bed, with RON helping him put the top half of his suit on – with pyjama bottoms. RON has the top half of his suit on too. THORN is agitated, wrestling with the clothes.

RON: Thorn, take it easy –

THORN: Get off, Ron.

RON: I'm only trying to help.

THORN: I know.

RON: I don't want to be best man if you don't want me to.

THORN: It's not that.

RON: I thought Bunny'd spoken to you –

THORN: This suit's wet.

RON: Always said you look good in a wet suit.

THORN: Lorna –

RON: Thorn, I don't think it's political to keep talking about Lorna.

THORN: I don't want to be here any more.

THORN pulls his bandage off his head.

RON: Your head –

THORN: My head doesn't hurt anymore.
It was the bandage that was hurting, not my head.
Not me.
I'm not hurting.

He tries to get out of bed – RON tries to get him in again, but THORN struggles to get up again.

RON: You're sick, Thorn.

THORN: Sick of all these coincidences and no conclusions, effect with no cause, meaning without motivation.

RON: I think you should sit down.

RON sits him down, but THORN is soon up again.

THORN: Seeing something happen to someone and telling someone about it and them telling me something that's happened to someone and everyone has their own small business and never does more than five minutes work because they're too busy arguing about their personal problems.

RON sits him down.

RON: Sit down.

THORN: And never being able to talk to someone without someone interrupting and having to make my point in less than five sentences to the same half dozen people I see at the same places every day. Why don't we ever go to a different café, Ron, and see different people?

RON: Sure we could do that, Thorn.

THORN is out of bed, in the top half of his suit.

THORN: Everyone always wanting to know where I've been, who I was with, who's on the phone.

RON: Stone the flamin' crows, mate –

THORN: Why is everyone watching me?

RON: No-one's watching you.

THORN: Why is no-one watching me? It's like Mum.

RON: It's not, Thorn.

THORN: Like it's all happening again.

RON: Don't spit the dummy – it's just a touch of last-minute nerves.

THORN: The lost and forgotten. That woman from the caravan park who fostered children.

RON: I wondered where she got to.

THORN: The Christian bloke who ran the guesthouse.

RON: Harry.

THORN: They're all out there. Mum. Harry. And Lorna.

RON: You've got to stop talking about Lorna.

THORN: And Peter – where's Peter?
I've got to get out of here.

As THORN's about to go, BUNNY enters with the buttonholes and a floral display.

BUNNY: Going somewhere, Thorn?

THORN: Bunny –

RON: Let me give you a hand –

RON takes things from her.

BUNNY: Call me Mother.

THORN: Mother.

RON signals to BUNNY that THORN's losing it.

RON: (*To BUNNY.*) Kangaroo loose in the top paddock.

BUNNY: I don't want any trouble, Thorn.

BUNNY exits again – RON pins a buttonhole on THORN.

RON: You're marrying Noleen.

THORN: Who's Noleen?

RON: She's the love of your life.

THORN: Just a centreless weave of hair and accessories.

RON: You two are the one sure thing round here.

THORN: Nothing's sure.
Not yet.

BUNNY enters with the arch and the cake, helped by a NURSE. RON takes the arch from her.

BUNNY: The vicar's arrived. Noleen's ready.

RON starts drilling the arch around THORN's bed, BUNNY arranges flowers and positions the cake.

RON: Won't be a tic.

BUNNY: Thank-you, nurse.

The NURSE exits. NOLEEN enters in her wedding dress.

NOLEEN: Shall I come in now?

BUNNY: No!

RON: Not yet, love.

NOLEEN exits back outside.

THORN: Where's Peter?

BUNNY: Perhaps he's not feeling so good.

THORN: That's not true.

BUNNY: Should never have come back from Brizzie, if you ask me.

RON: Sit down, mate.

He pushes him back onto the bed. NOLEEN enters again.

NOLEEN: When do I come in?

BUNNY: When I tell you.

NOLEEN: He's seen my dress now.

RON: Not really. He's not really looking.

BUNNY: Get out.

NOLEEN exits again.

A ninety-nine year old man like him shouldn't be travelling all over the place.

RON: Ninety-nine?

THORN: He's not ninety-nine.

RON: What's going on here, Bunny?

NOLEEN enters again.

NOLEEN: Have you started without me?

RON has finished the arch . The room is ready. PETER comes in and comes to speak to THORN – without anyone else noticing.

THORN: (*To PETER.*) Peter! Where did you come from?

PETER: (*To THORN.*) Don't worry about that now. I've found the cabin.

NOLEEN: Where's the vicar?

PETER: (*To THORN.*) It's on the beach.

NOLEEN: Ron?

THORN: (*To PETER.*) Lorna?

RON: Yes, sweets?

PETER: (*To THORN.*) It's buried in the sand.

NOLEEN: What's going on?

PETER: Quick –

PETER and THORN start to exit.

BUNNY: A wedding, Noleen, let's keep it simple.

BUNNY ushers NOLEEN off. RON finishes the arch.

RON: Right.

BUNNY: Here comes the bride!

THORN and PETER look at each other.

THORN: (*To PETER.*) Go –

PETER exits. RON manhandles THORN onto the bed. NOLEEN enters.

RON and BUNNY: Aah!

NOLEEN comes to sit next to THORN on the bed.

THORN: I can't marry Noleen.

BUNNY: Course you can.

NOLEEN: Thorn?

BUNNY: You're wearing a suit, she's wearing a dress.

THORN: I can't marry you.

NOLEEN: You said you loved me.

THORN: They were just words.

NOLEEN: All these years you said you loved me.

THORN: I don't know why I said them.

NOLEEN: I believed you.

THORN: I'm very fond of you, Noleen, and when so many people said how in love with you I was, I suppose I took it on board. But I can see now that that's not true.

NOLEEN: You're not who I thought you were.

THORN: And that any marriage between us will end in disaster, not because of any one thing either of us might do, but simply because this relationship has no foundation in any sort of reality.

BUNNY: No!

NOLEEN: I thought you were the man of my dreams.

BUNNY: You have to marry Noleen!

THORN: I'm sorry if I'm a disappointment to you, Noleen, but I think I always would have been, just as you – ultimately – would be for me.

BUNNY: You have to get married, Noleen –

NOLEEN: I don't have to do anything.

BUNNY: You do – you have to marry that man. It's all organised.

NOLEEN: I thought we'd always be together.

BUNNY: Your dress – my dress. Ron's suit.

RON: Thanks for noticing, Bunny.

NOLEEN: We were going to have children.

BUNNY: The flowers and the archway and the cake.

BUNNY picks up the cake.

RON: Thought I'd better spruce myself up a bit.

NOLEEN: What about our children?

BUNNY: What happens to me if you don't get married?

RON holds BUNNY by the shoulders.

THORN: We'd probably have developed some fertility problems and you'd end up getting pregnant to the high school headmaster.

BUNNY: Look at the cake!

NOLEEN: Mr Langridge?

BUNNY: Marry him, Noleen!

THORN exits.

NOLEEN: The only way I'll marry is for love and if he doesn't love me, then I'm not marrying him.

NOLEEN looks into the middle distance, gutted. BUNNY still holds the cake.

Scene Ten

Crystal Bay, the beach. The cabin of the Jack Rabbit is half-buried in the sand. As LORNA bangs on it – unseen from the other side – we see that it's jammed shut by the sand.

LORNA: (*From behind the door.*) Help me! Please, help me!

She shakes and bangs the door.

Nothing's going how it's supposed to.
Don't leave me here! Please!
Thorn!
Thorn – let me out!

After a bit more banging, she stops. Silence.

Scene Eleven

Arthur Street, the street. CHRIS and ANNABEL enter.

ANNABEL: She doesn't care who she hurts. She was never interested in you. You're just another sucker she reeled in and ripped apart.

CHRIS: Nothing you're saying means anything.

ANNABEL: But now you can do something about it.

CHRIS: Nothing we do means anything.

ANNABEL: She drove you to drink.

CHRIS: If it wasn't for my skin, I wouldn't know what's me and what's fresh air.

ANNABEL: Look at you. You're a mess.

CHRIS: I'm full of nothing.

ANNABEL: She's done that to you.

CHRIS: I'm a living balloon.

ANNABEL: You've been wearing the same clothes for days.

CHRIS: I don't know where my other clothes are.

ANNABEL: Here –

She gives him the keys to his truck.

CHRIS: What's that?

ANNABEL: The keys to your truck.

CHRIS: I've been drinking, Annabel.

ANNABEL: It doesn't matter.

CHRIS: I can't walk properly.

ANNABEL: You're beside yourself.

He looks beside himself, expecting to see himself there.

CHRIS: I shouldn't have had that half bottle of whisky.

ANNABEL: You didn't know what to do with yourself.

CHRIS: I'm way over the limit.

ANNABEL: That's the whole point.

CHRIS: Why?

ANNABEL kisses him.

Why do you keep doing that?

ANNABEL: You're going to get in your truck and when I say drive, you're going to drive.

CHRIS: Where's the truck?

She starts to guide him.

ANNABEL: It's over here.

He falls to the ground.

CHRIS: I can't.

ANNABEL: You have to.

CHRIS: No, I really can't.

ANNABEL snatches the keys.

ANNABEL: Give them to me.

ANNABEL exits, leaving CHRIS on the floor.

Scene Twelve

The Duke's – the cellar door. It is being pulled from the other side – sand being scraped from around the base. It starts to open.

PETER: That's it.

The door opens and PETER stands there. THORN looks over his shoulder.

THORN: Go on.

PETER: I'm not the right person for this.

THORN: Can we talk about that later?

PETER moves out of the way and THORN comes through.

PETER: What if I find Floss?

THORN: Are you looking for her?

PETER: I don't know if I'd even recognise her.

THORN rushes off.

Scene Thirteen

The hospital. NOLEEN is taking her wedding dress off.

NOLEEN: This was the one thing I was sure of.

BUNNY: Don't take the dress off, Nols.

As fast as NOLEEN is taking the dress off, BUNNY is putting it back on again.

NOLEEN: The one day I was sure I'd get.

BUNNY: (*To NOLEEN.*) We'll find him, Nol, and we'll change his mind.

NOLEEN: The happiest day of my life.

BUNNY: Where's Ron?

NOLEEN: He should have been my husband now.

BUNNY: We'll change his mind for him.

NOLEEN: We should be on our way to Bali now.

BUNNY: A lot of people have put a lot of effort into getting this wedding right.

NOLEEN: This isn't Bali.

NOLEEN has the dress on again – and starts to take it off.

BUNNY: A lot of people have stuck their necks out.

NOLEEN: Maybe you stuck yours out too far this time, but.

BUNNY: The wedding's going to happen.

NOLEEN: It isn't going to happen, Mum.

NOLEEN has the dress almost off.

BUNNY: Put the dress on.

NOLEEN: If you'd let him have it on the Jack Rabbit.

BUNNY: How could I? Neale put paid to that.

NOLEEN: It wasn't Neale.

BUNNY puts the dress back on – at moments, it looks like they're fighting.

BUNNY: Of course it was Neale.

NOLEEN: It wasn't, was it Mum?

BUNNY: So who was it?

They stop fighting over the dress. NOLEEN looks at her Mum.

Who was it, Noleen?

NOLEEN can't say.

This was my wedding too.
You fight for what you want in this life.
Or it's snatched away.
End up on your own. Out in the cold.
You got to fight a bit.
Put the dress back on, Nols.

She tries to put the dress back on NOLEEN.

I didn't know he was on it.
You heard him – he said he wasn't going on it.
He said he had things to do.
I wouldn't have done it if I'd have known he was on it, sweets.

NOLEEN: You know what I can see when I look in your eyes?
Granddad's house. My wedding dress. The Jack Rabbit.
All mixed up like a big cake but instead of me and Thorn it's you on top. You.

BUNNY: I was so careful.

NOLEEN: You never cared about me.

BUNNY: Always used protection.

NOLEEN: You never wanted children.

BUNNY: I didn't even have sex the month I caught with you. I don't remember the pregnancy. The first thing I knew was this crying thing thrust suddenly into my arms. And I was a mother.

NOLEEN: You weren't interested in me.

BUNNY: A mother. I didn't ever want to be a mother.

NOLEEN: You couldn't remember my name until you had it tattooed on your arm.

BUNNY: I thought if I got this marriage right and got rid of Granddad, I could get shot of you and get some limelight.

NOLEEN: You didn't want me.

BUNNY: You never leave me alone, Nols.

NOLEEN: You never wanted me.

BUNNY: I wanted to be a woman.
A gorgeous woman that everyone talked about. Forever.

NOLEEN walks out, still wearing the wedding dress, leaving BUNNY gob-smacked.

Scene Fourteen

Arthur Street, outside MARY's house. LORNA enters with a crow bar, to open the cellar door. FLOSS comes after her, with her trolley.

FLOSS: I regret I ever opened that door.

LORNA: You broke Peter's heart.

FLOSS: And you'll regret it.

LORNA: He still loves you.

FLOSS: I never asked him to.

We hear the truck start up and, as the scene continues, it approaches – headlights blaring.

LORNA: Don't you want to see him?

FLOSS: No.

LORNA: You gave away your own child.

FLOSS: It was a mistake. I was married.

LORNA: You were supposed to go away with him on the Jack Rabbit.

FLOSS: People like us only go out on boats when we're going to drown.

LORNA: We're going to get away.

FLOSS takes hold of the other end of the crowbar – pulling LORNA back.

FLOSS: Away where?

LORNA: Somewhere else.

FLOSS: There is nowhere else.

LORNA: If there is, I'll find it.

FLOSS: This is all there is.

LORNA: What if it isn't?

FLOSS: Our lives are all the same.

JOELY enters.

JOELY: Mum –

LORNA lets go of the crowbar.

I'm coming with you.

They embrace. THORN shouts, from off stage.

THORN: (*Off.*) Lorna!

LORNA: Thorn!

LORNA runs off after THORN.

JOELY: Mum!

JOELY runs off after LORNA.

CHRIS: (*Off.*) Annabel!

FLOSS: Lorna!

FLOSS runs off after JOELY and LORNA. A moment, then:

ALL: No!

The lorry sounds its horn. A cacophony of screeching and crashing and screaming plunges us into darkness.

Scene Fifteen

Bunny's. BUNNY stands, frozen with grief and terror, holding the wedding cake.

RON: You all right?

BUNNY: I've been looking forward to this day for so long.

RON: It's a very emotional time.

BUNNY: Everything in my life's always like this.

RON: What's the matter?

BUNNY: Like one of those shopping trolleys –

RON: Wheel bearings all shot, I know.

BUNNY: I'm trying so hard to steer it –

RON: Can't get any tracking if the bearings are worn.

BUNNY: I know where I want to get to –

RON: Only takes one wheel out of the four.

BUNNY: But no matter how hard I try it just keeps going in the other direction. Every time.
Why is it always me gets the dodgy trolley?

RON: Beautiful cake.

He puts the cake on the counter.

Come on.

BUNNY: I haven't been a very good mum. Don't like babies. And it wasn't Nol's fault she was a baby – she'd only just been born. I remember before I had her I was a young woman and it was like the moment they dropped her into my arms, I was a middle-aged woman.

BUNNY holds out one of her hands.

Young woman.

She holds out the other hand.

Middle-aged woman.

The first hand again.

Young woman.

Second hand.

Middle-aged.
And you can't seem to get back from that.

BUNNY looks into the middle distance.

Scene Sixteen

The street outside MARY's back door. LORNA holds THORN in her arms – he is badly injured. Blue lights flash. They change to beautiful pink, warm lights as the scene goes on. LORNA is very upset.

LORNA: Thorn – speak to me, Thorn – please – say
    something.
    Please.
    Don't do this to me.

She strokes his face.

Thorn.
You have to speak to me.

THORN is very calm.

THORN: I don't have to speak to you.

LORNA: This shouldn't have happened.

THORN: What else could have happened?

LORNA: Not to you.

THORN: I've lived like this for so long – if there's an out of control truck, you dive in front of it. It's all I know.

LORNA: All any of us know.
What are you thinking?

THORN: I don't have to tell you that.
I didn't have thoughts before we met.
Not proper ones that finished.

LORNA: I thought we could be happy.

THORN: It's a fleeting thing, Lorna.

LORNA: I don't want it to be fleeting.

A moment.

Where is everybody?

THORN: I suppose they're doing other things.

LORNA: Do you think something's happening somewhere?

THORN: I don't know.

They sit for a moment. FLOSS comes onto another part of the stage with her trolley, still wearing the rubber gloves, followed by JOELY.

JOELY: He just wants to talk to you.

FLOSS: No.

JOELY: He's come such a long way.

FLOSS: You don't know the first thing about me and Peter.

JOELY has hold of FLOSS' trolley. FLOSS won't let go of it and they wrangle as they speak.

JOELY: Let him see you.

FLOSS: I can't see him.

JOELY: Let him see you.

FLOSS: I can't look at him. He'll hate me.

JOELY: (*Calls off.*) Peter?

FLOSS: No!

JOELY exits. FLOSS hides. Back to LORNA and THORN. THORN is dying.

LORNA: What are we going to do?

THORN: We don't have to do anything, Lorna.
We don't have to discuss everything that happens.
We don't have to go to the same places every day. See the same people.
We don't have to have marriages that end badly.

LORNA: Or children who turn out not to be ours.
We don't have to be impossible bundles of contradiction in a world where everything about you has changed except your preference in soft drinks. And everyone's always having a row or a knees up or a punch up or a drink.

THORN is dead.

Thorn?

PETER enters. He sees FLOSS' trolley. He goes over to it. PETER speaks to FLOSS, not knowing where she is.

PETER: Floss?
You know I waited for you.
I waited even though I knew you weren't coming.
And I still loved you.
Even though you never came.
I love you because after I met you, nothing was the same.

He takes the ring box from his pocket.

Floss, I've got something for you.

FLOSS' hand – in a rubber glove – appears from her hiding place. PETER puts the ring on her finger. They exit.

LORNA: I don't have to say: 'What time did you come back last night?'. I don't have to say: 'You won't believe what's happened'. I don't have to talk about her wayward son. Or fancy Chris. Or run a pub. I don't have to have brassy streaks in my hair. None of it matters.

And things that do not matter will seep into the ground, and the words that mean nothing will be eaten by the air around them, and the thoughts that have no end will not begin, and events that are not necessary will fold in on themselves, and days that have been wasted will be crushed between two nights.

And in the space that's left I will see myself.

Lights down.